The Collected Works of
James M. Buchanan

VOLUME 5
The Demand and Supply of Public Goods

James M. Buchanan, Charlottesville, Virginia, 1964

The Collected Works of

James M. Buchanan

VOLUME 5

The Demand and
Supply of Public Goods

LIBERTY FUND

Indianapolis

First published in 1968 by Rand McNally & Company

| 05 | 04 | 03 | 02 | 01 | C | 6 | 5 | 4 | 3 | 2 |
| 04 | 03 | 02 | 01 | 99 | P | 5 | 4 | 3 | 2 | 1 |

Library of Congress Cataloging-in-Publication Data
Buchanan, James M.
The demand and supply of public goods / James M. Buchanan.
p.   cm. — (The collected works of James M. Buchanan ; v. 5)
Originally published: Chicago : Rand McNally, 1968.
Includes bibliographical references (p.   ) and index.
ISBN 0-86597-221-4 (hard : alk. paper). — ISBN 0-86597-222-2
(pbk. : alk. paper) 1. Public goods.   I. Title.
II. Series: Buchanan, James M.   Works.   1999 ; v. 5.
HJ193.B83   1999
336—dc21   98-43536

LIBERTY FUND, INC.
8335 Allison Pointe Trail, Suite 300
Indianapolis, IN 46250-1684

Contents

Foreword

In the fifteen years immediately following World War II, unquestionably the most significant development in public economics was the emergence of "public expenditure theory." This development arose in the attempt to define a comprehensive theory of the state around the notion of "market failure." For public economics, this was a significant development because, until that time, analysis focused on the tax side of the budget. Most of public economics could aptly be called "public finance" because the central preoccupations revolved around how "best" to raise the revenue required for public activities—public activities whose rationale lay entirely outside economic scrutiny. There were, to be sure, hints of what such a rationale might look like, for example, Pigou's famous treatment of the "smokey factory." But these hints remained partial and disparate until Paul Samuelson, in what became a famous series of articles on "public goods," set out what purported to be a coherent and synthetic justification for governmental intervention in economic processes. Samuelson provided an account of what James M. Buchanan was later to refer to as the "productive state."[1] In the Samuelson formulation, the critical element in this justification is the market failure that public goods give rise to in an extreme form. In this sense, public goods are a kind of distillation of various possible barriers to the market's capacity to exploit all the possible gains from exchange—gains that might in principle be appropriated by the citizens who compose the relevant group-polity-nation. The 1950s and

1. Paul A. Samuelson, "The Pure Theory of Public Expenditure," *Review of Economics and Statistics* 36 (November 1954): 387–89; "Diagrammatic Exposition of a Theory of Public Expenditure," *Review of Economics and Statistics* 37 (November 1955): 350–56; and "Aspects of Public Expenditure Theories," *Review of Economics and Statistics* 40 (November 1958): 332–38. James M. Buchanan, *The Limits of Liberty: Between Anarchy and Leviathan* (Chicago: University of Chicago Press, 1975), volume 7 in the series.

1960s saw a huge burgeoning in the normative analysis of markets, most of it oriented toward showing some market failure, so understood, and often associated with a putative case for some form of governmental intervention.

It is now folklore that the normative thrust of public goods analysis was an important element in the birth of the public choice movement. One central ambition of public choice scholarship was to insist that "political success" needed to be demonstrated before the market failure in question could establish a preference for government activity—and to demonstrate that such political success might be more difficult to achieve than the public economics presumption might suggest. Put another way, market failure was itself assessed by reference to a benchmark that economists came to understand only by contemplation of market operation in other (private goods) arenas. Market failure on its own meant nothing: Politics would have to submit to the same test. This much is familiar. And Buchanan's work has been critical in making it so.

It is, however, important to note that the public choice tradition has never denied the logic of the market failure argument as such. Indeed, Buchanan himself made extremely significant contributions to the market failure–public goods literature. For example, what are almost certainly Buchanan's two most famous articles—"Externality," with W. C. Stubblebine, and "An Economic Theory of Clubs"—fall precisely into this area of inquiry. In fact, public goods theory constituted a major (perhaps the predominant) element in Buchanan's research agenda throughout the 1960s. *The Demand and Supply of Public Goods* is to be seen as an important part of that body of work and should be read alongside the articles in volume 15 in the Collected Works, *Externalities and Public Expenditure Theory,* as Buchanan's attempt to synthesize and focus his views on those "public goods" issues. *The Demand and Supply of Public Goods* should perhaps also be read alongside the earlier contributions of Samuelson and Richard A. Musgrave. John G. Head provides a survey of this literature contemporaneous with *The Demand and Supply of Public Goods* that includes an article-length review of Buchanan's book.[2]

---

2. James M. Buchanan and W. C. Stubblebine, "Externality," *Economica* 29 (November 1962): 371–84; James M. Buchanan, "An Economic Theory of Clubs," *Economica* 32 (February 1965): 1–14. Both papers are included in volume 15 in the series, *Externalities and*

It is interesting specifically to contrast Buchanan's approach with the earlier Samuelson exposition. Two features are notable. First, whereas Samuelson's central purpose is to establish "optimal conditions" for the supply of public goods, and to show thereby that the Pareto optimum could never be a market equilibrium, Buchanan seeks to derive that market equilibrium directly. Such derivation is necessary to Buchanan's broad purpose of explicitly comparing market performance with political performance: Buchanan has much less interest in conceptually possible but institutionally infeasible ideals. Second, and related, much of Buchanan's treatment reads like a purely positive account of institutional choice. The quest for mutual advantage through exchange—whether a two-person exchange as for ordinary private goods or a many-person exchange as in the public goods case—serves in *The Demand and Supply of Public Goods* as a motivator of action as well as a relevant normative test. Accordingly, *The Demand and Supply of Public Goods* is an important piece of Buchanan's contractarian theory of the "productive state" with the ambiguity between the positive and normative use of the contractarian approach deliberately allowed full rein.[3] The contrast with Samuelson's much more overt (if incomplete) normative treatment, with the independently derived "social welfare function" as an express articulation of the "ethical observer's optimum," is worth noting. In this respect, Buchanan is much more faithful to the Wicksellian approach than is Samuelson, although both Samuelson's and Buchanan's treatments of the public goods question derive ultimately from Wicksellian sources. (In Samuelson's case, the derivation is through Musgrave's paper on Erik Lindahl's version of Knut Wicksell's analysis.)[4]

And it is worth emphasizing that Wicksell's original contribution repre-

---

Public Expenditure Theory. James M. Buchanan, *The Demand and Supply of Public Goods* (Chicago: Rand-McNally, 1968), volume 5 in the series. Samuelson, "The Pure Theory," 387–89; "Diagrammatic Exposition," 350–56; and "Expenditure Theories," 332–38; Richard A. Musgrave, *The Theory of Public Finance* (New York: McGraw-Hill, 1959). John G. Head, *Public Goods and Public Welfare* (Durham: Duke University Press, 1974).

3. Buchanan, *Limits of Liberty,* 1975, volume 7 in the series.

4. Richard A. Musgrave, "The Voluntary Exchange Theory of Public Economy," *Quarterly Journal of Economics* 53 (February 1939): 213–37; Erik Lindahl, *Die Gerechtigkeit der Besteuerung* (Lund: Gleerupska Universitets-Bokhandeln, 1919); Knut Wicksell, *Finanztheoretische Untersuchungen* (Jena: Fischer, 1896).

sents the origin of public choice to politics as well as the point of departure for subsequent literature on public goods and market failure. It is therefore unsurprising that Buchanan, for whom the Wicksell influence is more explicit, should have made independent contributions in both areas and been a determined proponent of their inextricable connections.

The particular occasion for writing the first draft of *The Demand and Supply of Public Goods* was a series of lectures given at Cambridge University in 1961–62. The audience originally conceived for the book was therefore a group of relatively able undergraduate and graduate students. But little of the flavor of a textbook is detectable here—there is no dry pedagogy and surely no concession to the undergraduate concentration span. What Buchanan provides here is a clear statement of the contractarian approach to public goods problems, very much in the "voluntary exchange" tradition of Wicksell and Lindahl.

GEOFFREY BRENNAN
Australian National University
1998

Preface

The title, "The Demand and Supply of Public Goods," has been selected to emphasize those features that set the book apart from orthodox public finance and at the same time tie it to neoclassical economics. Public finance, traditionally, has neither contained a theory of demand nor one of supply. Public goods and services have not been central to this subdiscipline. Public finance has been rather straightforward applied price theory, and its scientific content has been limited to predictions about the reactions of individuals and firms to fiscal institutions. The scholar from outer space, coming to earth in the post-Marshallian era, might have concluded on perusing the English-language literature that governments exist wholly apart from their citizens, that these units impose taxes on individuals and firms primarily to nourish the state; and he might have thought that positive public finance consists in predicting the effects of these taxes. Normative public finance, observed alongside the positive elements, consists in pronouncements about how taxes *should* be imposed.

Marshallian economics is essentially a theory of the demand for and the supply of private goods, and of the institutions (markets) through which exchange takes place. Traditional public finance has been applied Marshallian economics with a liberal side dosage of utilitarian nonsense. The linguistic provincialism of English-language scholars precluded familiarity with early continental attempts to extend economic theory to public as well as to private goods. The words of Sax, Pantaleoni, de Viti de Marco, Mazzola, Erik Lindahl, and, most importantly, Knut Wicksell remained almost wholly ignored in English and American writings before World War II.

Through the work of R. A. Musgrave, Howard Bowen, Paul Samuelson, J. G. Head and others, this deficiency has been overcome to an extent during the last quarter-century. A theory of the demand for and the supply of public goods and services has emerged, built on the foundations of the late-nineteenth-century continental efforts, and this theory is now beginning to find its place in the elementary public-finance textbooks, especially those that have been written since the mid-1950s. No independent and systematic exposition of the theory has appeared; this provides the motivation for the present book.

The analysis is necessarily different even if not difficult, and there need be no pretense that this is an elementary textbook of the standard sort. A degree of sophistication in economic analysis is required and some familiarity with the content of theoretical welfare economics should prove helpful. I have tried, where possible, to present the analysis carefully. Although no claims are made concerning new theory here, my own insight and arrangement of the theoretical structure differ from those of some other scholars in the field. To this extent, the treatment is uniquely mine, and no attempt is made to assume a position of methodological objectivity. No claims are made concerning absence of analytical error here. The theory has not yet become received doctrine. For this reason, it remains interesting, but, by the same token, the theorist is likely to blunder.

The book is based on materials that I have presented in a second-year graduate seminar at the University of Virginia from 1957 to 1968. These materials have been modified each year, I hope with gradual improvement. They were first written up in manuscript form in the fall of 1961, when eight lectures were delivered at Cambridge University, where I spent the 1961–62 academic year. The version presented here was actually written during the 1964–65 and 1965–66 academic years, and the summer of 1966. Final revisions were made in late 1966 and early 1967.

The weekly papers that I have required of students in the graduate seminar were essential building blocks in the analysis. My indebtedness to all who participated should be acknowledged, especially in view of the apparent stress on analytical trivia often suggested in the assigned topics. Among the many participants in this seminar over the decade, particular note should be made of Thomas Borcherding, Otto A. Davis, Emilio Giardina, Charles Goetz, Mark Pauly, Charles Plott, Craig Stubblebine, and Richard Wagner, almost all of whom made postdoctoral, postcritical comments on earlier drafts of the full manuscript. Helpful advice for revision also came from J. G. Head of Australian National University, Milton Kafoglis of the University of Florida, David

Davies of Duke University, and, at many stages, from Gordon Tullock of Rice University. Detailed and helpful comments for revision were also provided by Tibor Scitovsky, who provided the encouragement to get this book in published form. Mrs. Betty Tillman deserves far more than the usual acknowledgement of appreciation for secretarial assistance, from me especially, but also from all who participated in the community of scholarship that characterized Rouss Hall in the 1960s. Funds made available through a National Science Foundation grant supported my work during the summer of 1966. I should also acknowledge with appreciation the assistance of Subrata Ganguly in preparing the Index.

J. M. B.
Charlottesville
February, 1967

The Demand and Supply of
Public Goods

1. A Methodological Introduction

People are observed to demand and to supply certain goods and services through market institutions. They are observed to demand and to supply other goods and services through political institutions. The first are called private goods; the second are called public goods.

Neoclassical economics provides a theory of the demand for and the supply of private goods. But what does "theory" mean in this context? This question can best be answered by examining the things that theory allows us to do. Explanation is the primary function of theory, here as everywhere else. For the private-goods world, economic theory enables us to take up the familiar questions: What goods and services shall be produced? How shall resources be organized to produce them? How shall final goods and services be distributed? Note, however, that theory here does not provide the basis for specific forecasts. Instead, it allows us to develop an explanation of the structure of the system, the inherent logical structure of the decision processes. With its help we understand and explain how such decisions get made, not what particular pattern of outcome is specifically chosen.

This process of explanation involves several stages. There is first a set of conjectural predictions, a set of basic behavioral hypotheses, or laws. These may be wholly conjectural, requiring the mental feat of constructing the pound of *ceteris paribus.* On occasion, hypotheses may be derived that involve empirically testable implications, and when data can be assembled properly evidence may be adduced in corroboration or refutation. This strictly positive content of economic theory has, perhaps, been somewhat overemphasized in recent years to the partial neglect of theory's more basic function. This is the development of the logical structure of an economy through the making of what may be called inferential predictions. The trained economist can predict the general shape or pattern which tends to emerge from the exchange or market process. These predictions are not of the conditional "if *A* then *B*" variety, at least not in any directly analogous sense. Instead, these generalized predictions take the form, "*A* tends to equal *B*." The distinction here between elementary conditional predictions and inferential predictions has not been fully appreciated, perhaps because both are present in the central body of economic theory.

Conditional predictions take the form: If price falls, quantity demanded increases; if price increases, quantity supplied increases. All such conditional predictions, whether empirically verifiable or not, are combined to generate a logical structure for the whole system of behavioral interactions that we call the economy. To the extent that the conditional predictions in the set are valid, inferences may be drawn concerning the general characteristics of the outcomes that will emerge. These inferences are also predictions, and they are essentially descriptive in nature. They provide information about the relationships among variables: Prices will equal costs; wage rates for similar workers will be equalized; factors of production will earn their marginal product.

A vital link in the logical chain between conditional and inferential prediction has been deliberately omitted in the above sketch. Assume that the conditional hypotheses of the economist are valid. That is to say, the predicted behavioral responses are correct. Individuals will buy more goods when prices fall; firms will supply more goods when prices rise, etc. It is impossible to move from this knowledge directly to the statement that "prices will tend to equal costs," until and unless we postulate something about the institutional-organizational structure within which individuals are allowed to make choices. Orthodox procedure in this respect has been that of explicitly or implicitly postulating competitive organization. Once this missing step is added, the inferences about results or outcomes follow logically from the set of conditional hypotheses. The descriptive characteristics of the results can be indicated.

In their most sophisticated form, these characteristics are presented as the familiar statements for the necessary marginal conditions for efficiency or optimality, the presumed domain of theoretical welfare economics. It is important to note that these conditions are inferential predictions and that they are positive in content, given that competition is postulated as the organizational structure. These conditions become conceptually refutable predictions about the descriptive characteristics of the results of the market interaction process. No normative elements need be introduced.

The weak step in this methodological procedure is the assumption that must be made about institutional-organizational structure. Only to the extent that this assumption is relevant will inferences be corroborated. As an example, consider the economist faced with predicting the effects of the 1965 excise tax reductions in a particular industry. Assume he predicts that prices will fall to a certain degree; his predictions are, we shall say, refuted by events. Does this refute the underlying conditional hypothesis that firms in the industry are profit-maximizers, or does it, instead, refute the hypothesis that the industry is competitively organized? Clearly, it may do either, or neither if still other relevant variables have changed. The standard procedure of assuming competitive order when this seems convenient is not acceptable. Appropriately thorough analysis should include an examination of the institutional structure itself in a predictive explanatory sense. The economist should not be content with postulating models and then working within such models. His task includes the derivation of the institutional order itself from the set of elementary behavioral hypotheses with which he commences. In this manner, genuine institutional economics becomes a significant and an important part of fundamental economic theory.

If human interaction is limited to voluntary exchange conceived in its broadest sense, a theory of institutional structure can be derived, yielding something closely akin to the standard model of competitive order as the end or equilibrium product. In other words, a somewhat loosely defined competitive economic organization can be predicted to emerge from the play of human interaction so long as this interaction is limited to voluntary exchange. Using nothing more than his standard tools, the economist can predict, first, the emergence of this structure, and, secondly, the characteristics of the outcomes that such a structure will tend to produce.

Only after this stage is reached can the economist begin to talk about the relationship between competition as an organizational structure, and efficiency. No criteria can be externally introduced. Efficiency becomes a descriptive term that is used to specify the existence of certain relationships among variables and among institutions which are produced through the process of voluntary exchange. The satisfaction of the necessary marginal conditions for efficiency, viewed in this light, becomes a prediction of results that will tend to emerge from the exchange process, not a criterion for telling us what should be present in order to further some externally derived value norm. The derivation of these necessary conditions, and of the institutional structures that will cause them to be satisfied from the choice processes of individuals engaging mutually in trade, is the central task of economic theory. When observed results appear to counter those predicted, either in terms of specific characteristics of outcomes or in terms of institutional structure, explanation of divergence becomes a supplementary and proper task. And analysis, here as elsewhere, must proceed simultaneously at several levels.

Theory of Public Economy

The extended methodological digression on the function of orthodox economic theory in application to the private economy is designed to provide some assistance in discussing the analogous role of theory as extended to the public economy, to the demand for and the supply of public as opposed to private goods. At base, the economist must begin from the same set of conditional hypotheses. He deals with the same individuals as decision-making units in both public and private choice, and, initially at least, he should proceed on the assumption that their fundamental laws of behavior are the same under the two sets of institutions. If he predicts that the average or representative person will purchase a greater quantity of private good A when the relative price of A is reduced, he should also predict that the same person will "purchase" a greater quantity of public good B when the relative "price" of B is lowered. This step in itself represents a significant departure from orthodoxy in public finance. Individual behavior patterns in demanding public goods, in participating in political decision processes, in voting, have not been examined in detail by economists (or by anyone else). A body of theory devoted to individual participation in voting processes is only now emerging. And even here, the individual's behavior in demanding public goods, as some functional relationship between quantity demanded and the "tax-price" that he pays, has not been studied either analytically or empirically. Even more dramatic departures from public-finance orthodoxy are required, however, when inferences as to results are drawn. There is nothing analogous here to the competitive model, the use of which so greatly facilitates our elementary textbook predictions concerning the outcomes produced under voluntary exchange processes in the private-goods sector.

As suggested above, many economists have more or less jumped over the step of institutional theorizing in their analysis of markets, perhaps without fully realizing that they have done so. They are able to do this because the competitive-model assumptions yield predictions about outcomes that are not dramatically at variance with observation, tending thereby to corroborate both the assumptions and the conditional hypotheses. Despite all of the discussion about the unrealism of these assumptions, they remain paradigmatic for economists. Decisions on the demand-supply of public goods are made through political, not market, institutions, and there is no analogue to competitive order that eases the analytical task.

There are two possible ways along which the analyst might proceed. First, a specific political decision structure can be postulated and inferences made concerning the pattern of results that will emerge. Alternative models can be tried, and various differences in predictions noted. This approach has much to recommend it. However, nothing can be said about efficiency in this framework.

The second approach is that of making an attempt to derive the institutional structure from the broadly conceived exchange process. The economist can try to predict, as best he can, what sort of political decision structure will tend to emerge from the voluntary "political exchanges" that may be entered into by rational persons. Once this decision structure is derived, he may be able to characterize outcomes of actual processes in a manner that is analogous to his treatment of the private-goods sector. To a limited extent, the term "efficiency" may be introduced to describe certain outcomes, with this term having essentially the same meaning as that which applies in the private-goods world.

There must remain, however, an important difference in the degree of relevance that theory has in the two sectors. As Wicksell so perceptively noted, outcomes or results of individuals' choices for public goods in discrete instances can only be classified unequivocally as efficient or optimal by some external observer if group decisions are made under some effectively operating rule of unanimity. For discrete allocations, political-choice institutions embodying decision by unanimity become the analogue to market-choice institutions that are described as perfectly competitive. In both cases, we are dealing with idealizations. For the latter, however, observed interactions seem to produce proximate realization, and the ideal commonly becomes, in one sense, the accepted norm for policy changes. That is to say, the institutions of the competitive market economy have been widely accepted to be desirable, over and above their place in the analysis which suggests that these describe the structure that would tend to emerge, ideally, from the free workings of voluntary exchange processes. Presumably the costs of achieving some approximation to the ideal here are not considered sufficiently high to warrant significant modifications in the norm, although some of the discussions of workable competition may be so interpreted. It is for this reason that efficiency conditions applicable to the private-goods economy have been widely understood as carrying important normative implications. And the very use of the emotive words "efficiency" and "optimality" tends, of course, to reinforce this interpretation.

I have suggested above that the familiar conditions need not embody such normative implications. Basically, they represent nothing more than inferences drawn from the set of hypotheses that make up economic theory, inferences that describe certain results that will tend to emerge from the interaction of many separate persons in voluntary exchange processes, including the institutions themselves as variables subject to choice. The drawing of such inferences, which are themselves predictions, remains within the scope of positive economic theory, and hence within the professional competence of the economist. He can, and should, say nothing whatever concerning the desirability of such outcomes or such institutions as might generate these outcomes.

The barrier between positive theory and normative advice must always be vigilantly maintained. It is difficult to accomplish this separation even in the strict private-goods world, as the discussion here suggests. Theoretical welfare economics, as a subdiscipline, is considered by many economists, perhaps by most, to involve necessarily normative elements. As I have tried to indicate, however, the fundamental content of this subdiscipline can be incorporated into positive theory with no normative overtones.

The same barrier between positive and normative theory is much more difficult to maintain when the demand-supply of public goods is introduced. Here the role of theory seems much more limited, and the analysis much less relevant to the observed world. The theoretical idealization analogous to the competitive order, that represented by Wicksell's unanimity rule for making group choices, is sufficiently removed from real-world experience so that it rarely serves even as a norm for policy action. Presumably, by contrast with the private-goods sector, the costs of attempting to approximate the ideal here are considered to be so great that wholly different norms must be introduced.

Properly conceived, however, theory can do precisely what it can do in the private-goods world. It can describe, and at several levels, the outcomes that will tend to emerge from the process of voluntary exchanges among individuals. It can do no more than this, and the economist has no role in pushing further. By the nature of the different universe that he confronts, the limits of theoretical relevance for the economist seem to be reached much earlier here. In a genuine sense, all discussions of political-decision rules can be interpreted as treating of "workable unanimity," but the distance between the ideal and the alternatives that seem plausibly possible is so great as to cause the ideal itself to lose apparent relevance.

The reason is not difficult to find. A community of individuals decides to demand goods and services publicly through governmental-political processes, rather than privately, precisely because the bilateral exchanges facilitated by market arrangements are insufficiently inclusive. External effects are exerted on parties other than those directly entering into the market exchange, and these effects are considered to be relevant and important. "Exchanges," trades, agreements among all members of the community are deemed more efficient by these members. Multilateral agreements are, however, far more costly to negotiate than bilateral ones. In addition, the incentive for initiating negotiation leading toward agreement in such cases may be absent. These facts are evident to such an extent that it often appears as folly to make any attempt to examine the outcomes that genuinely voluntary exchange processes would produce in the theoretical idealization described by the unanimity rule. The limits of the voluntary exchange theory of the demand for and the supply of public goods are indeed narrow, especially when compared with its analogue, the theory of perfectly competitive markets.

The exercise is nonetheless useful, and it does provide the only available "pure theory" of public finance, upon which all derivative theoretical constructions rest. By first ignoring the costs of negotiating n-person agreements, by ignoring the absence of individual incentive to organize agreements in the

n-person case, the theorist can proceed with his description of the results of idealized political process. These descriptions are wholly analogous to those made about results of market processes that are characterized by perfectly competitive conditions. The statements of the necessary conditions for efficiency are closely similar in the two cases, and in neither is normative content necessary. The satisfaction of the necessary marginal conditions may or may not represent desirable social objectives, and it is not the role of the economist to make such a determination.

One of the primary purposes of this book is that of stating these conditions and examining their implications. The theory is intended to be positive, and its extremely limited relevance is recognized and acknowledged. It is the "pure voluntary exchange theory of public finance" and is presented for the simple reason that this theory must first be developed rigorously before we can begin to examine more relevant models. Again the theory is on all fours with that of perfectly competitive markets; only after the latter was fully worked out could more refined analysis begin. In specific terms, the theory presented in the early part of this book describes the results that the political process would produce if a general rule of unanimity should be operative. The treatment here is in the strict Wicksellian tradition, and is, in fact, Wicksell revisited or modernized.

Initially, the costs of negotiating n-person agreements are largely ignored. In a broader framework, and at a later stage, these costs must be introduced since they are essential to an understanding of the public economy. Analysis at this second stage must incorporate the costs of reaching agreements, or making collective decisions, and an economic theory of political constitutions developed. The individual's own recognition that, in the public-goods world, he is likely to be caught in an n-person analogue to the prisoners' dilemma will prompt him to agree to "workable unanimity" rules. He will trade off some efficiency (as measured by the standard criteria) in exchange for more efficient decision-making. The whole theory of political order becomes directly relevant to the demand and the supply of public goods, inclusively considered.

The analysis is developed progressively from the simplest models to complex ones. Chapter 2 examines the demand-supply of a single pure public good in the highly restricted two-good, two-person, world-of-equals model. Only the world-of-equals assumption is dropped in Chapter 3. The purity of the public good is abandoned in Chapter 4, and the analysis is extended to a many-person group in Chapter 5. The novel world where all goods are public is treated in Chapter 6. The problems presented by the publicness of any political decision are introduced in Chapter 7, and the specific institutions of fiscal choice are considered in Chapter 8. The interesting and important question that has been assumed to be central in much of the modern theory, Which goods should be public? is examined in Chapter 9. Suggestions for a positive theory of public finance are advanced in the concluding chapter.

For those students and scholars who do not fully share the methodological approach that I have suggested, and whose interests lie primarily in the derivation of the necessary conditions for Pareto efficiency or optimality in the public-goods sector, most of the analysis is applicable and relatively straightforward. To an extent, my treatment can be interpreted within this framework as an alternative version of the normative theory of the public sector in the Samuelson-Musgrave tradition.

One additional and final point should be made in this introductory chapter. The demand for and the supply of public goods are discussed throughout the book under the assumption that the community contains a specific number of persons. I shall neglect in this book the important set of issues that is introduced when attempts are made to determine efficient or optimal sizes of membership in sharing groups. I hope to develop some of the analysis of these issues in a later work.

2. Simple Exchange
in a World of Equals

In this chapter we shall examine the demand and the supply of public goods in the simplest of models, one in which there are only two persons and two goods, one public and one private. To make simplicity absolute, we assume initially that the two persons are identical, both as to productive capacity and as to tastes. For convenience, we shall name these two persons Tizio and Caio, adding a touch of Italian flavor to the analysis. We may think of these two persons as being the only inhabitants of an island in the tropics. This allows us to use coconuts as the purely private good. Coconuts are available to each person upon a specific outlay of time spent in gathering them, and this outlay per coconut gathered remains constant over relevant quantities. Mosquito repelling is the other good (service), and this is purely public or purely collective. That is to say, the death of one mosquito benefits each man simultaneously, and is thus equally available to each man. The service of mosquito repelling is also continuously variable, and specific quantities can be secured by certain outlays of time on the part of either person. The cost per unit of output remains constant over relevant quantities.

Our purpose is to examine the process through which equilibrium in the demand and the supply of both the private and the public good is attained, and to define the characteristics of this outcome which will tend to emerge from the simplified two-person exchange process.

Independent Adjustment

Examine first the situation in which the two persons act independently, which would be the case if neither Tizio nor Caio recognizes that mosquito repelling activity exhibits publicness. Each would then consider this activity, along with that of gathering coconuts, as purely private, and under the conditions we have assumed (equal tastes, equal productive capacities, constant returns) there would be no incentive to engage in trade. Each man would proceed to reach a wholly private position of equilibrium without trading with the other. The preliminary position sought for by each person would be equivalent to that which would be attained in the one-person world.

Each man's preferences for the two goods can be depicted on an orthodox indifference map which is derived from a standard utility function. This construction for one man is shown in Figure 2.1, on which units of the public good are measured along the vertical axis and units of the private good along the horizontal axis. The opportunities open to the individual are limited by his capacity to locate coconuts on the one hand and his capacity to repel mosquitoes on the other. These opportunities are summarized in the transformation function, which by our simplified assumptions is linear, drawn in Figure 2.1 as *PP*. The individual will initially seek to attain position *E*. He will fail to reach this point, however, because in his calculus he does not, by our

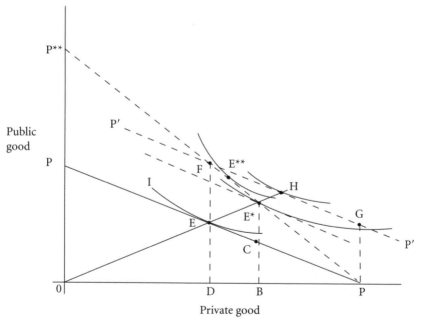

Figure 2.1

assumption, take into account the publicness of the one good. Because of this publicness, the activities of the two persons will necessarily be interdependent.

In attempting to attain position E, the person will actually reach F because his fellow will be making an outlay on mosquito repelling precisely equivalent to his own. Since, by definition, the public good or service is equally available to both persons, no matter by whom produced, the individual will find himself with a bundle that contains double the amount of the public good that he anticipated in making his initial decision to commit resources.

F is not a position of final equilibrium, however, except under the highly restrictive condition where the income elasticity of demand for the private good is zero. Finding himself at F, the individual will consider it advantageous to change his plans. He will treat the newly found public good as a simple increase in his opportunities, in his real income, although the rate at which he can change one good into the other will not be modified. In making new plans, the individual will try to adjust to his apparent transformation curve $P'P'$.

Normally, he will reduce somewhat his production of mosquito repelling and expand his production of the private good, coconuts. In the extreme case where the income elasticity of the public good is zero, he would seek to attain an adjusted position at G. If both goods exhibit positive income elasticity, the second sought-for position will fall somewhere between F and G. For simplicity, assume that the income elasticity of the public good (and, in the two-good model, for the private good also) is unitary. In this case, the second-round objective under wholly independent adjustment would be shown by H.

This position will not be attained and for the same reason that E was not attained; the activities of the two persons are interdependent. Adjustments will continue to take place until a position at E^* is reached, which will represent one of final equilibrium under wholly independent behavior. Note that, geometrically, E^* is located where BC is equal to CE^*. By our assumption of unitary income elasticity the position of equilibrium is located along the ray EE^*H.

In describing the adjustment toward this final equilibrium we have assumed that the publicness of the one good remains wholly hidden from the individuals in the model. This insures that there is no strategic behavior in the adjustment process. Tizio does not recognize that Caio's efforts provide him with benefits; therefore, he has no incentive to modify his own behavior in the hope of securing more of the external economies.

Under the conditions assumed and with the utility function as depicted in Figure 2.1, the introduction of strategic behavior on the part of one or both of the persons will not modify the location of the final equilibrium position. This is insured by the fact that the position of equilibrium, E^*, lies on a higher utility level than G, the extreme position that might be sought, and potentially attained, by one of the two individuals who behaves strategically. As the construction makes clear, however, this ordinal relationship between E^* and G need not be present, even in the two-person model. If this relationship is reversed, and if one of the persons succeeds in reaching G while the other remains in E, a nonsymmetrical equilibrium of sorts is achieved. Although the active strategist will not be in full marginal adjustment, he will recognize that some concealing of his true preferences remains optimal.

The construction of Figure 2.1 can be used to demonstrate that the independent-adjustment equilibrium is nonoptimal in the Pareto sense. Both persons adjust to the apparent production-possibility curve through E^* parallel to PP. Under genuine joint or cooperative behavior, the actual production-possibility curve faced by each person is shown by PP^{**}. Although the individual cannot act independently on the basis of this production-possibility set, simultaneous action on the part of both persons will allow each to move along PP^{**}, finally attaining the optimal position, E^{**}. The next section discusses the attainment of this full equilibrium under exchange agreements.

Trading Equilibrium

The characteristics of any equilibrium depend upon the institutions under which the private behavior of individuals takes place. In the initial model, all behavior was assumed to be independent; no exchange or trade, no mutual agreement, no negotiation or bargaining, were allowed. If these restrictions are dropped and the rules or institutions changed so as to allow personal interaction, the position attained under wholly independent adjustments will not remain one of equilibrium.

Each man will now recognize that mosquito repelling is a genuinely collective activity, and that there exist unexploited mutual gains from some trading arrangements that insure a larger total outlay on the provision of this service. Simple two-person, two-commodity trade is impossible, however, since both men enjoy identical quantities of the public good. What can be traded or exchanged here is some *agreement* on the part of each man to contribute working time (labor) toward the production of the collective good, in this example, mosquito control. Tizio can "buy" Caio's agreement to kill mosquitos (1) by agreeing to kill mosquitos himself, and/or (2) by transferring to Caio a quantity of coconuts, the purely private good. The two alternatives will be wholly indifferent to both men under the simplified conditions postulated. If the two men should differ in productive capacity, however, or if there should be returns to scale in the production of either good, comparative advantage in the ordinary sense would determine the efficient trading arrangements. Should Tizio be relatively more efficient in locating coconuts, he would spend all of his time in this way, and then he would "purchase" the public good solely through maintaining Caio's private-goods consumption. Should Caio, by contrast, be relatively more efficient in coconut gathering, he would provide some private-goods subsistence for Tizio, while the latter carries out the public activity of killing mosquitoes.

The process through which trading equilibrium comes to be established may be shown in Figure 2.2, which is an Edgeworth-box diagram converted for current purposes. Here we measure Tizio's labor time spent in gathering coconuts *for his own consumption* on the horizontal axis, and Caio's time spent in gathering coconuts for his own consumption on the vertical axis. We assume that each man has available a fixed quantity of labor time to devote to the production of goods, public or private, and that this time is identical for each man. In effect, we assume that leisure is not a variable in the model. In the orthodox sense, the origin for Tizio is at 0, that for Caio at $0'$.

We now define point A as that position attained under the wholly independent adjustment process previously discussed. Hence, $0A$ is the amount of time that Tizio spends in gathering coconuts in the private-adjustment equilibrium; similarly, $0'A$ is the time Caio spends on the same activity. Confronted with the private production-possibility curves indicated by P, both persons are in equilibrium at A.

With this construction it becomes possible to generate an indifference map for each man that will indicate his tastes for the public good and the private good, but in such a way that exchange can be analyzed. The individual's eval-

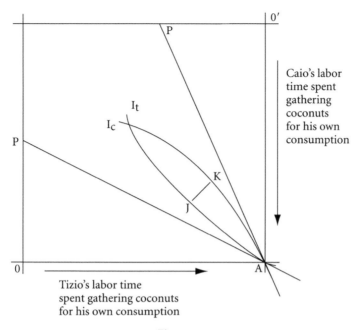

Figure 2.2

uation of the public good can be considered as an indirect evaluation of his fellow's labor time spent in producing the good. Any upward vertical movement in Figure 2.2 represents, for Tizio, an increase in the quantity of the public good supplied because, as Caio gives up gathering coconuts for his own use, he must either (1) devote his time to mosquito control, or (2) gather coconuts for Tizio's use. Similarly, any leftward horizontal movement on Figure 2.2 represents, for Caio, an increase in the quantity of the public good that is supplied to him (as well as to Tizio). Mutually beneficial exchange can obviously take place so long as the movement from *A* is in the general northwesterly direction. The position of trading equilibrium will be located at some point along the contract locus, *JK*, in Figure 2.2. At this final equilibrium, both Tizio and Caio will be giving up a specific amount of their own time to the production, directly or indirectly, of the public good. And more of the public good and less of the private good will be supplied than at *A*.

Bargaining strength and luck may, of course, determine the shares of the two men in public-goods production, within limits. Since mutual gains are secured in the shift from the no-trade position at *A* to a position on the contract locus, there exist many possible distributions of these gains over infra-marginal ranges. This may, because of income effects, generate slight differences in the quantity of the public good, but these can be neglected here.

We may now examine carefully the characteristics of the position of full trading equilibrium; that is, any point on the contract locus, *JK* in Figure 2.2, where trade has stopped and all further prospects for mutual gains are eliminated. By the standard geometry, we know that the indifference curves of the two traders are tangent; in this respect the position is similar to that reached when trade takes place in purely private goods. This tangency condition indicates that the marginal rates of substitution between the two items traded are equal for the two persons. Let us define these marginal rates of substitution precisely.

Tizio is giving up units of private good, coconuts, in exchange for units of public good, mosquito repellent, as the latter is reflected in Caio's willingness to "supply" the second good, either through his own labor or through providing Tizio with subsistence. Caio is in a similar position on the other side of the exchange. There seems to be something wrong here, however, since *both* men value the public good, and *both* must adjust to the *same* quantity, by definition. Something different from simple two-person, two-commodity trade must be taking place. The mystery here, if indeed there is one, is resolved when we recognize that all exchange is two-sided. If there is a demander there must also be a supplier. Hence, one or both of the two traders in our model must be supplying the public good or service to the other who is demanding it. Let us continue, for now, to assume that there is no comparative advantage, that each man produces an equal share of the public good that is jointly consumed by both. Each man, therefore, is "supplying" units of the public good to the other, in exchange for a similar supply on the part of his trading partner. Equilibrium is defined by the standard equivalence between marginal rates of substitution. But what this definition masks, in its simple form, is the evaluation that each man himself places on the public good that he himself supplies to the other. In this setting, Tizio is supplying Caio with units of public good, but in the process, he is also supplying himself. His marginal rate of substitution is a summation of two separate components. He must consider his own marginal evaluation of the public good, purely as a consumption item, plus his negative marginal evaluation of the same good as this arises from his share of the supply or production cost.

This somewhat particularized interpretation of trading equilibrium is made necessary by the publicness of one of the traded goods. The analysis may be clarified if we assume that one of the two traders does possess a comparative advantage over the other in producing the public good. Let us suppose that Caio can produce mosquito repellent at a relative advantage over Tizio. The trading process will then lead to Caio supplying all of the public good and receiving from Tizio a certain quantity of the private good in order to maintain his own consumption of the latter. In full trading equilibrium, Tizio's standard marginal rate of substitution in consumption between the two goods will be equated to Caio's marginal rate of substitution *in exchange.* The latter will include two components, Caio's own marginal rate of substitution in consumption between the private and the public good, and his own marginal rate of substitution between the two in production. This point will be further clarified in the simple algebraic treatment of the model in the next section.

Algebraic Statement of Trading Equilibrium

The simple Tizio-Caio model of two-person, two-good trade when one of the two goods is purely public can now be discussed with elementary algebraic tools. Any complexities that arise in this section will be clarified in subsequent discussion. Essentially the same formal analysis introduced here is again presented for the more general case at the end of Chapter 4.

Tizio's utility function is defined as

$$U^t = U^t (x_1^t, x_2^c, x_2^t), \tag{1}$$

where X_1 is the private good (coconuts) and X_2 is the public good (mosquito repellent). Superscripts designate the person who produces the goods in question, directly or indirectly. Caio's utility function is defined in the same way as

$$U^c = U^c (x_1^c, x_2^c, x_2^t). \tag{2}$$

For simplicity, we continue to assume that each man devotes a fixed amount of labor input to total goods production, public and private.

Each man will confront a transformation function indicating the rate at which the private good can be converted into the public good, and *vice versa,* through his own behavior. These transformation functions are

$$F^t = F^t(x_1^t, x_2^t); \tag{3}$$

$$F^c = F^c(x_1^c, x_2^c). \tag{4}$$

If each man acts independently, and no trade takes place, equilibrium will finally come to be attained when the conditions indicated in (5) and (6) below are met. In writing these conditions, we adopt the convention of using lower-case u's and f's to indicate the partial derivatives of the utility and transformation functions respectively, with goods noted in the subscripts and persons in the superscripts. Thus,

$$\frac{\partial U^t}{\partial x_1} \Big/ \frac{\partial U^t}{\partial x_2}$$

is written as

$$u^t x_1 / u^t x_2.$$

$$\frac{u^t x_2^t}{u^t x_1^t} - \frac{f^t x_2^t}{f^t x_1^t} = 0; \tag{5}$$

$$\frac{u^c x_2^c}{u^c x_1^c} - \frac{f^c x_2^c}{f^c x_1^c} = 0. \tag{6}$$

These conditions are the standard ones for individual marginal adjustment; each person modifies his own behavior so long as the marginal rate of substitution in consumption differs from his marginal rate of transformation.

We now want to see why trade takes place, how it takes place, and what equilibrium will tend to emerge.

We know from the definition of a public good that a unit of x_2 produced and consumed by Tizio is valued by Caio to the same extent that he values a unit of his own production. Similarly, for Tizio's evaluation of a unit produced and consumed by Caio. This guarantees that, in the no-trade equilibrium, Tizio's activity in producing the public good exerts a Pareto-relevant external economy on Caio, whereas Caio's activity in producing the public good exerts a similar externality on Tizio. Each person values the producing activity of the other at some value greater than zero in the no-trade equilibrium. No value will be placed by either man on the production of private goods by the other. In algebraic language, these conditions may be stated

$$\frac{u^t x_1^c}{u^t x_1^t} = 0, \quad \frac{u^t x_2^c}{u^t x_1^t} > 0; \tag{7}$$

$$\frac{u^c x_1^t}{u^c x_1^c} = 0, \quad \frac{u^c x_2^t}{u^c x_1^c} > 0. \tag{8}$$

Each person places a positive value on the marginal extension of public-goods production by the other. Each will, therefore, be willing to "pay for" this extension, and, in response, each will stand willing to extend his own production for any receipt above zero. Trade will, of course, take place under such conditions, and will continue until (9) and (10) below are satisfied.

$$\frac{u^t x_2^c}{u^t x_1^c} = (-)\left[\frac{u^c x_2^c}{u^c x_1^c} - \frac{f^c x_2^c}{f^c x_1^c}\right]; \tag{9}$$

$$\frac{u^c x_2^t}{u^c x_1^t} = (-)\left[\frac{u^t x_2^t}{u^t x_1^t} - \frac{f^t x_2^t}{f^t x_1^t}\right]. \tag{10}$$

As stated in (9) and (10), the conditions are fully general for two-person, two-good exchange, and these same statements encompass any degree of externality or "publicness" in x_2. For example, suppose that x_2 has been erroneously labeled as being purely public when, in fact, both Tizio and Caio consider it to be purely private. In this case, the left-hand terms in (9) and (10) become zero; the no-trade position is restored. Trade will not emerge under the restricted conditions of this example where the two persons are identical with respect to tastes and productive capacities and where production functions are constrained. As a second example, suppose that x_2 is only partially public; that is to say, Tizio values his own mosquito repelling activity more than he does the similar activity of Caio, although he places some positive valuation on the latter. Conditions (9) and (10) are not modified; they remain those that must be met in full trading equilibrium. Or, to take a less familiar variation, suppose that *both* x_1 and x_2 are purely collective. Conditions (9) and (10) continue to define equilibrium in the two-person, two-good case. However, as we shall introduce at a later point, the generalization here to three or more persons becomes different from that in models where at least one purely private good exists.

If we postulate at the outset that one of the two goods is purely public, as we have done in this chapter, it becomes possible to simplify greatly the statement of the necessary conditions for equilibrium. This simplification has been implicit in most of the statements made by those scholars who have been instrumental in developing the modern theory of public goods. When x_2 is known to be purely public, these necessary conditions can be reduced to (9) alone if the assumption is made that only one of the two persons produces the public good. Suppose that Caio actually produces this good, and that Tizio pays him for the appropriately determined share through a transfer of private goods. This allows us to transpose and to drop the now unnecessary sub- and superscripts to get

$$\frac{u^t x_2}{u^t x_1} + \frac{u^c x_2}{u^c x_1} = \frac{f x_2}{f x_1}, \tag{9A}$$

which can be readily recognized as the familiar definition of the conditions for public-goods optimality, as presented by Paul A. Samuelson and others. The summed marginal rates of substitution between the public good and the private good must be equal to the marginal rate of transformation, or, somewhat loosely, marginal cost.

Note that, as these have been discussed here, the conditions (9), (9A) and (10) have not been explicitly connected with "optimality" or "efficiency." These conditions are presented as those which allow us to define the characteristics of an equilibrium position, one that will tend to emerge from a two-person trading process. Until and unless these are satisfied, mutual gains from further trade can be shown to exist. In such situations trade will take place, provided that we ignore, as we shall throughout most of the elementary analysis, the costs of negotiating market agreements themselves.

Some Marshallian Geometry

One of Professor Frank Knight's favorite quotations is from Herbert Spencer's Preface to the *Data of Ethics:* "Only by varied iteration can alien conceptions be forced on reluctant minds." Since the analysis attempted here qualifies as alien, at least to some degree and to some students, I shall heed Spencer's advice, even at the expense of redundancy. Having presented the theory of simple exchange in one of the most sophisticated of the economist's several languages, I shall now discuss the same material with more mundane tools. Some rigor is necessarily lost in the process, and the logic becomes imperfect in its details. Elementally, however, the principles that emerge are not modified, and considerable gain may be registered toward genuinely intuitive understanding of the exchange process.

The tools that are most familiar to traditional micro-economists are the geometrical constructions of Marshallian demand and supply, and these can be employed here in analyzing trade or exchange in the mixed world that contains both private and public goods. For expositional simplicity, it is necessary to neglect income-effect feedbacks on individual marginal evaluations of the public good. We assume continuous variation in the quantities of the two goods. Under these conditions, it becomes possible to derive a single marginal evaluation schedule or curve for the public good, measured in units of the private good, a schedule or curve that will not shift as a result of changes in the distributions of the net gains-from-trade in the public good. Such a curve is plotted as E in Figure 2.3. Because of our assumption that Tizio and Caio are identical with respect to both tastes and productive capacities, the construction is simplified greatly. This allows us to utilize the same marginal evaluation curve for each person. We can also draw in a curve that measures the marginal cost of producing the public good. For simplicity, we assume this to be uniform over varying quantities; this is drawn as MC in Figure 2.3.

In complete independence of the other person's activity, Tizio and Caio

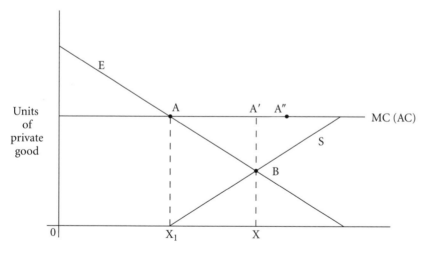

Quantity of public good

Figure 2.3

would each aim initially at reaching the position shown at *A*. In trying to do so, however, each would find himself at *A″*, where double the amount of public good anticipated is available for his own consumption. At this juncture each person will have a strong incentive to cut back on his own production of the public good. This is because, at the consumption margin, the marginal evaluation placed on the good falls below the marginal cost of producing it. If action takes place instantaneously, costlessly and simultaneously, we could expect both persons to cease production, each expecting the other to provide the public good in the desired quantity. Under these extreme conditions, we should expect a cyclical pattern of behavior, between no production of the public good and an excessive amount. It seems reasonable here to make the model somewhat less restrictive by assuming that there will be some departure, however slight, from absolute simultaneity in adjustment.

Let us suppose that Tizio, having tried to attain position *A*, finds himself in position *A″* slightly before Caio realizes that he too is in a similar position. This differential in response time allows Tizio to adjust to the external economy that Caio exerts upon him before the latter reciprocally reacts. Tizio will immediately reduce his own production of the public good. In the case where income effects are neglected altogether, he will reduce his own production completely, to zero. Once he has done so, Caio has no incentive to reduce his own production below $0X_1$, assuming away strategic considerations. Each person would then find himself in private-adjustment equilibrium. Caio, who has initially tried to reach position *A*, finds himself where he expected to be. He still secures some "consumer's surplus" despite the fact that he is the only producer. Tizio, having adjusted most quickly, enjoys the full benefits of the public-goods quantity $0X_1$ without cost. He secures a larger consumer's surplus than Caio. However, Tizio has no incentive to expand his own output above zero.[1] Caio has no incentive to reduce his below $0X_1$. If trade is prevented, and if strategic behavior is absent, equilibrium is attained.

Strategic behavior may, of course, arise to disturb this equilibrium, even if trade is prevented. If each person recognizes the interdependence that the publicness of the one good necessarily introduces, he will be led, especially in a two-person or small-number setting, to behave strategically. Each man

---

1. This model differs from that discussed in connection with Figure 2.1 because of our neglect of income effects here.

may find it sensible to hold off production, even below the levels that seem privately rational, in anticipation of tricking the other partner into taking on the lion's share of the costs, as Caio has done in our illustration. This whole matter of strategic behavior, which is closely related to what has been called the "free-rider problem," is very important in the theory of public goods. We shall devote considerable space to a discussion of this problem at a later point in this book. At this early stage, it seems best to leave the matter out of account, since it does not modify the characteristics of equilibrium that is attained after trade takes place, and it is these characteristics, and not the means of getting to equilibrium, that are the primary subject of attention here.

We now want to demonstrate why and how trade will take place, starting from the position of independent adjustment equilibrium. Tizio and Caio are both in private equilibrium, with Caio producing an amount, $0X_1$, of the public good; Tizio produces nothing; both persons consume the full amount produced by Caio. Figure 2.3 allows trade to be depicted readily.

Caio finds himself at position A; Tizio finds himself in the same position, but without having undergone any cost. The potentialities for mutually advantageous trades become apparent when we ask the question: How much will Tizio be willing to pay Caio for the latter's agreement to produce additional units of the public good? And, on the other side, how much will Caio have to receive in order that he express some willingness to produce additional units? If the first answer involves a number no smaller than the second, trade will tend to arise. The roles of the two persons in the questions could be reversed, of course, with Tizio rather than Caio taking on the marginal or incremental production.

Note that, beyond A, Caio still places a positive marginal evaluation on the good, as shown by the curve, E, to the right of A. He need only receive, as a minimum, the *difference* between this marginal evaluation and the marginal cost of producing. In this way, it becomes possible to construct a *supply curve* for incremental production beyond the amount $0X_1$. This is derived geometrically by subtracting vertically the evaluation curve, E, from the marginal cost curve, MC. This supply curve is labeled S in Figure 2.3.

How much will Tizio be willing to pay Caio for the latter's offer to undertake additional public-goods production? This is shown by Tizio's own marginal evaluation of the quantities beyond the amount $0X_1$. Trading equilibrium is attained when demand equals supply, or at position B, where the output $0X$ is produced, in this illustration wholly by Caio, and is consumed by both persons. At this trading equilibrium, the amount that Tizio is willing to pay Caio for the marginal extension of production is just equal to the minimal amount that Caio is willing to accept. There remain no unexploited gains-from-trade at the margin of adjustment. By our neglect of income effects, the distribution of the inframarginal gains-from-trade does not modify the position of trading equilibrium. Over the range of production between $0X_1$ and $0X$, such gains may be shared in any one of many ways, depending on the relative bargaining strengths and skills of the two traders.

In this illustration, we have assumed that Tizio is the initial free rider and that trade involves his payment to Caio for additional production. This assumption does not modify the analysis. In the movement from no production to the final position of trading equilibrium, significant gains are realized. These may be distributed in many ways. At every point, some bargaining range will exist, and the outcome of the two-person bargaining negotiations will determine the subsequent path toward final equilibrium. Because of our explicit neglect of income-effect feedbacks on individual marginal evaluations, the same quantity of public good will be produced in full trading equilibrium regardless of the route taken to attain this equilibrium. If we drop this simplifying assumption, the geometry becomes messy and difficult to handle, but the characteristics of the final trading solution remain essentially the same. In this case, however, the equilibrium quantity of the public good may be modified somewhat by the route through which this equilibrium is attained.

The characteristics of the final equilibrium position are those defined in the conditions (9) and (10) of the preceding section. In full trading equilibrium, the marginal rate of substitution between the public good and the private good in consumption, indicated by the marginal evaluation curve, minus marginal cost to the individual, either incurred through producing the good himself or through paying or receiving subsidies from his trading partner, must be zero for each person. Referring again to conditions (9) and (10), these may be rewritten in the measurements of Figure 2.3 as follows:

$$BX = (-) [BX - A'X];   (9\text{-}2.3)$$

$$BX = (-) [BX - A'X].   (10\text{-}2.3)$$

In the more familiar language of the modern theory of public goods, which implicitly assumes that only one person produces all of the public good, we can say that the summed marginal rates of substitution equal the marginal cost of, in terms of Figure 2.3,

$$2BX = A'X, \qquad\qquad (9 \text{ A-2.3})$$

which is, of course, the same condition restated.

Bibliographical Appendix

The theory of private-goods exchange is rigorously developed in Peter Newman's book [*The Theory of Exchange* (Englewood Cliffs, N.J.: Prentice-Hall, 1965)]. Although his analysis is presented axiomatically, his procedure in moving from the simple to the more complex trading models closely parallels that which is followed in this book.

To my knowledge, the theory of public goods has not been presented in terms of the simple models of two-person exchange developed in this chapter, although the "voluntary exchange theory," especially in the Erik Lindahl formulation, can be interpreted in this way [*Die Gerechtigkeit der Besteuerung* (Lund, 1919), translated as "Just Taxation—A Positive Solution," and included in *Classics in the Theory of Public Finance*, edited by R. A. Musgrave and A. T. Peacock (London: Macmillan, 1958), pp. 168–76]. The basic Lindahl model has been interpreted in modern terms by Leif Johansen ["Some Notes on the Lindahl Theory of Determination of Public Expenditures," *International Economic Review*, IV (September 1963), 346–58].

The independent-adjustment outcome in the presence of public-goods phenomena has been discussed by James M. Buchanan and Milton Z. Kafoglis and by Buchanan and Gordon Tullock [Buchanan and Kafoglis, "A Note on Public Goods Supply," *American Economic Review*, LIII (June 1963), 403–14; Buchanan and Tullock, "Public and Private Interaction Under Reciprocal Externality," in *The Public Economy of Urban Communities*, edited by J. Margolis (Resources for the Future, 1965), pp. 52–73].

Although they are not directly relevant to the elementary discussion of this chapter, the basic contributions to the modern theory of public goods first of all by Knut Wicksell and then by Paul A. Samuelson and R. A. Musgrave should be cited early, along with the valuable survey papers by J. G. Head [Wicksell, *Finanztheoretische Untersuchungen* (Jena: Gustav Fisher, 1896), a major portion of which is translated as "A New Principle of Just Taxation," and included in *Classics in the Theory of Public Finance*, edited by R. A. Musgrave and A. T. Peacock (London: Macmillan, 1958), pp. 72–118; Samuelson, "The Pure Theory of Public Expenditure," *Review of Economics and Statistics*, XXXVI (November 1954), 387–89; "Diagrammatic Exposition of a Theory of Public Expenditure," *Review of Economics and Statistics*, XXXVII (November 1955), 350–56; Musgrave, *The Theory of Public Finance* (New York: McGraw-Hill, 1959), especially Chapter 4; Head, "Public Goods and Public Policy," *Public Finance*, XVII (No. 3, 1962), 197–221; "The Welfare Foundations of Public Finance Theory," *Rivista di diritto finanziario e scienza delle finanze* (May 1965)]. In his monograph, Kafoglis also provides a useful summary of the theory [*Welfare Economics and Subsidy Programs*, University of Florida Monographs in Social Science, No. 11, Summer 1961]. In his introduction to the second edition of his book, William J. Baumol summarizes recent developments in the theory of public goods in the context of general developments in theoretical welfare economics [*Welfare Economics and the Theory of the State*, Second edition (Cambridge: Harvard University Press, 1965), pp. 1–48].

In papers that have come to my attention only after the manuscript of this book was substantially in its final form both Samuelson and Musgrave re-examine and reinterpret their own earlier contributions. In the process, several ambiguities are clarified [Samuelson, "Pure Theory of Public Expenditure and Taxation" (Mimeographed, September 1966); Musgrave, "Provision for Social Goods" (Mimeographed, September 1966)]. Both of these papers were prepared for the Biarritz conference organized by the International Economic Association, and, presumably, they will appear eventually in the published conference volume.

3. Simple Exchange
in a World of Unequals

The several simplifying assumptions that have been imposed on the models of simple exchange have been aimed at laying bare the essentials of the trading process. The characteristics of equilibrium can be generalized since these do not depend on the particular restrictions imposed on the models. Complexities have been obscured in the elementary treatment, however, and it is time to commence the laborious, but fascinating, task of dismantling the simplifications one by one.

The most vulnerable of these involves the complete identity of our two potential traders. Let us start the dismantling process by dropping only the restriction that the two persons in the model have identical preference functions, identical tastes. How will this single change modify our analysis? We adopt methodological partial differentiation here, and keep all of our other assumptions inviolate. We remain in the two-person, two-good world; we assume identity in productive capacity, with simple linear transformation functions. We assume away strategic behavior, and neglect income-effect feedbacks.

In reference to the tools previously introduced, we shall start here in reverse order, with the Marshallian geometry. The construction developed in Figure 2.3 can be readily adjusted to allow for differences in tastes between the two persons in the group. Figure 3.1 illustrates this. Two marginal evaluation curves must now be drawn, one for each person. The curve for Tizio is labeled E_t; that for Caio is labeled E_c.

In ignorance of the public-goods interdependence, Tizio would aim at producing the quantity $0X_t$ anticipating a private consumption of like amount. Caio would, in the same situation, aim at producing the quantity $0X_c$. Let us again assume as we did in the earlier illustration, that Tizio recognizes and

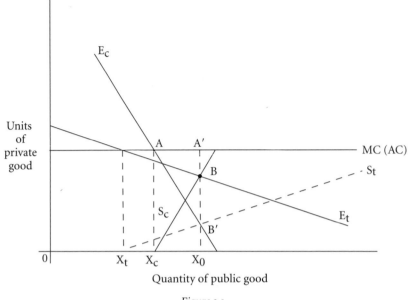

Figure 3.1

acts on the interdependence sooner than Caio. As he does so, he will be motivated to reduce his public-goods production to zero. He will enjoy his "free ride" from the spillover benefits, the external economy, generated by Caio's production. Caio, waking up somewhat later to the essential interdependence, will find himself at *A,* precisely where he expected to find himself in the absence of the interdependence.

The prospects for trade and the position of final trading equilibrium can be shown as in the discussion of Figure 2.3. Beyond the quantity $0X_c$, Tizio will stand ready to subsidize Caio for additional production in the maximum amounts indicated by the curve, E_t, to the right of *A.* Caio in turn will be willing to supply additional units of the public good, for joint consumption, at marginal supply prices indicated by the curve S_c. This curve is derived by subtracting vertically Caio's own evaluation curve, E_c, from the marginal cost curve, *MC.* Trading equilibrium is attained at position *B,* or at public-goods quantity $0X_0$. At the margin, Tizio pays BX_0 in exchange for Caio's agreement to produce the indicated extension in quantity of the commonly shared good. Caio, in accepting this subsidy which is lower than the marginal cost of production, is himself "paying for" the public good, at the margin, a marginal "price" of $A'B$.

This construction can be modified without difficulty to allow Tizio to become the marginal producer of the public good. His supply curve, in the marginal sense, becomes S_t, and the point of intersection between this curve and the evaluation curve for Caio, E_c, determines trading equilibrium, shown at B'. This is precisely the same public-goods output as that shown at B; only the roles of the two traders have been reversed. At the margin, Tizio is now paying $A'B'$, which, by construction, is equal to BX_0. Caio is paying $B'X_0$, which is equal to $A'B$.

Under the assumption that neglects income-effect feedbacks, the quantity of the public good is not modified by the way in which the two traders grope their way toward final equilibrium. If this income-effect feedback is introduced, the distribution of the net gains to be made from trade over inframarginal units will shift marginal evaluations, and the final position may depend, to a degree, on the precise manner that equilibrium is approached. Again this modification would not change the essential characteristics of the final equilibrium position.

The basic difference between the outcome that emerges in this world-of-unequals and that which was shown to emerge in the world-of-equals is found in the distribution of costs at the margin between the two traders. In the world-of-equals, the model showed the obvious; the cost of the public good must be shared equally at the equilibrium margin of adjustment. This remains true regardless of the possible differentials in the distribution of total costs due to bargaining luck over the inframarginal trading ranges. If we should allow the income-effect feedbacks, this result would not have been forthcoming, since these effects alone would make for differences in the two traders, and would, in one sense, violate the world-of-equals model even with the assumed identity of tastes and productive capacities.

When tastes are allowed to differ, even if we disregard the income effects, this symmetry in marginal-cost shares no longer holds, nor should we expect it to hold. As the construction suggests, shares in the costs of producing the public good at the margin where all trading gains are exhausted will be dependent on the respective marginal evaluations that are placed on the quantity of the good.

Differential Marginal Prices for Public Goods

Only in this unequals model does one of the important differences between equilibrium characteristics in an economy with public goods and those in an economy where all goods are purely private become crystal clear. In the standard neoclassical setting where all goods are privately divisible, all purchasers face the same marginal prices when full equilibrium has been established. What is the basis for this important difference?

With privately divisible goods, a difference in marginal price as between any two persons represents a trading opportunity that remains unexploited. The person confronted with the higher of two prices can gain by purchasing the good through the offices of the person who confronts the lower price. The former will gladly pay something for this unexploited avenue for trade, over and above the external price confronting the latter. And the latter will gladly undertake the indirect purchase for some payment beneath the price that confronts the former. In such situations, price differentials cannot exist except insofar as they reflect genuine "equalizing" differences, in which case they should not be called differentials.

In the case of public goods, no such retrading is possible. By definition, these goods are not privately divisible. Individually, persons cannot adjust their own purchases over varying quantities. The same quantity must be available for each member of the relevant group. But different persons will place different marginal values on any given quantity. If each person is to be in equilibrium in the sense that, for him, the quantity supplied is that which he prefers, differentials in marginal prices must be introduced. And, as the simplified analysis has already indicated, such differentials will come to be established through the processes of trade or exchange.

This interesting difference between equilibrium states in the world of private goods and the world of public goods is worth further examination. What are the dimensions of the quantity units in each case?

Units of Consumption and Units of Production

With privately divisible goods, as these are ordinarily conceived, it is not necessary to answer the question posed above. The unit that is produced or supplied is dimensionally equivalent to the unit that is consumed by some ultimate buyer. A single unit of production implies the availability of a single unit for consumption, by some one person. And this person's ultimate act in consuming the unit removes all possibility of others' like consumption of the same unit. It is the absence of this one-to-one relationship that is the basis of the public-goods distinction. With a pure public good, a unit that is produced or supplied is, by definition, simultaneously available for the consumption of all members of the relevant group. Hence, a unit that is supplied is wholly different in dimension from a unit that is consumed. The consumption of a unit by one person does not reduce or remove the possibility of consumption by another person.

This may be put in terms of our simple illustration. A single unit of public-goods supply, mosquito repellent, amounts to two units of consumption, one for Tizio and one for Caio. Care must be taken to keep this dimensional difference in mind; otherwise confusion can easily arise when we discuss some of the complexities in later parts of this book. For example, many economists have referred to the public-goods interdependence as an example of extreme external economies *in consumption.* This usage is misleading for the standard illustrations. There need be no external economy stemming from the *act* of consuming the good on the part of one individual or the other. The spillover benefit, the external economy, may arise wholly from the act of *producing* the good that is *commonly consumed.* Note that genuine external economies in consumption can arise, and some of these will be discussed briefly at a later point, but these are not the standard examples for pure public goods. At this early juncture, our interest is restricted to the classic illustrations, e.g., lighthouses, police and fire protection, mosquito control.

Marshall's Theory of Joint Supply

When it is recognized that the unique element in a public good, as contrasted with a purely private good, is the common sharing of a *jointly supplied* unit, we can examine neoclassical economic theory to see what analogies to the modern theory of public goods might have been developed. The theory of joint supply that is found in Marshall's *Principles* is, in its fundamental respects, equivalent to the theory of public goods. This suggests that there may be precious few principles in economics after all.

Marshall conceived his theory in application to physical commodities that could be privately consumed, and there was no joint sharing of final consumption units in his models. For the Marshallian theory the jointness of supply arises because of the technological conditions of producing, not because of the technological conditions of consuming, as in the public goods case. However, as we shall demonstrate, the results that emerge from analysis are identical in the two models.

His classic example involved the joint supply of meat and leather, to which he added wool and mutton, wheat and straw. (The relevant discussion here is found in Alfred Marshall, *Principles of Economics,* 8th Edition, pp. 388–390, and Mathematical Note XVIII, p. 854.) The producer or supplier of bullocks simultaneously meets two separate demands, that for meat and that for leather or hides. These final products, desired by different demanders, are jointly supplied in the process of breeding and growing steers, necessarily so, under Marshall's initial assumption that the relative proportions of the final products in each unit of supply are fixed. Meat and leather are, of course, demonstrably different products at the stage of final demand, different in a superficially descriptive sense. The single unit of supply embodies two separate units of consumption. And no observing economist would predict that the equilibrium price for the meat contained in one bullock (the unit of supply) need be equal to the equilibrium price for the hides contained in the same bullock.

We can review Marshall's analysis by converting it into our own, Tizio-Caio model of two-person, two-good exchange. Assume, as before, that both persons produce and consume coconuts privately. For our second good, however, let us now substitute bullocks for mosquito repellent. Tizio, we shall say, uses hides for clothing; Caio has no use for hides at all. On the other hand, Caio eats meat; Tizio does not. Under these assumptions, the jointly supplied unit is, in effect, a purely public good because of the technology of production. Strictly speaking, we should also require the additional restriction that withholding of unused product is somehow impossible. Note that the problem in this converted Marshallian supply situation has become in almost all respects identical to that discussed in the earlier mosquito repellent illustration. The fact that, at the final or ultimate stage of consumption, the consumption units appear descriptively different in one model and similar in the other is irrelevant. In equilibrium, Tizio's demand price for leather or hides plus Caio's demand price for meat, both defined in terms of the quantities contained in the unit of supply, must just be equal to the marginal supply price of the jointly-produced unit.

This example can be readily discussed in terms of the geometry of Figure 3.1. In that construction, we did not draw in a combined or aggregate demand curve, derived by a vertical summation of the two separate marginal evaluation curves, but, had we done so, this aggregate curve would have cut the marginal cost curve at A'; the position of equilibrium determined in this way would have been identical with that previously discussed. If we think of the public good as being produced by third parties, external to our two persons (or two groups of demanders) this alternative construction which employs the summed marginal evaluation curves becomes somewhat more meaningful. In such a model, Tizio and Caio trade, not with each other alone, but with some external supplier of the public good, and the analysis becomes almost purely Marshallian.

Concentration on the Marshallian theory of joint supply allows several features of the public-goods problem to be clarified. First of all, Marshall's treatment, in its strict sense, depends for its validity on the assumption that supply is genuinely joint. If the proportions of meat and hides can be modified by the producers of steers, the analysis becomes considerably more difficult. With the public-goods model, however, this requirement of technological jointness in production is not required. If we define a good to be purely public, the analogue to fixity in proportions is guaranteed. The equal availability of the *same* quantity of the good, measured in units of supply, to all persons precludes any shifting in proportions. The relevance of this characteristic of public goods, which we may call extreme nonexclusion, may be questioned. As we shall demonstrate in a later chapter, however, *any* good or service can be treated as a purely public good, provided that it is organized through an institutional structure embodying the extreme publicness features. Technological characteristics of production or consumption need not be present for the analysis to be germane to the real-world fiscal structure as this structure, in fact, operates.

Marshall used his theory of joint supply to make predictions. He predicted that, under the restrictions of his model, a decrease in the demand for meat would tend to increase the equilibrium price for hides. We can do precisely the same thing with our public-goods model. In the two-person case, let us suppose that Caio becomes partially immune to mosquito bites; his demand for the commonly shared good falls. As a result, in any new equilibrium position, Tizio must contribute a larger cost of producing the good at the margin of adjustment. Or, conversely, suppose that Caio's demand should increase. Here, equilibrium output of the public good will increase and Tizio will find himself paying a somewhat lower marginal price.

Predictions of this nature have relevance beyond the oversimplified models that we have introduced. For instance, assume that the demand for publicly financed education on the part of one social group decreases. Pressures will be generated toward reducing the quantity of publicly supported educational services, and those groups whose demands have not fallen will find themselves subjected to pressures to pay increased school district rates. In such real-world settings, of course, "full trading equilibrium" may never be achieved or even approximated for many reasons. Nonetheless, the analysis of such equilibria is helpful in enabling the competent theorist to identify those political pressures that will arise concerning changes in the size of the budget and in the distribution of the tax burden.

Marginal Prices, Average Prices and Interpersonal Discrimination

There is one difference between the Marshallian model of joint supply and the public-goods model that is of some significance. As presented by Marshall, and as normally discussed, the joint-supply analysis is illustrated with reference to final-product components that are subject to retrade or resale among potential purchasers. Because the jointness arises in the technological process of production itself and not in the absence of divisibility or possibility of exclusion in the consumption of final products, the purchaser of a component of the jointly supplied composite may undertake resale to a third party if this offers opportunity for profit. This characteristic insures that an element of determinacy is present in the Marshallian model which is lacking in the public-goods model. Since resale is possible, prices of final product components must be uniform both over varying quantities of purchase for any one buyer and over separate persons as buyers. This implies that the attainment of a set of equilibrium marginal prices also determines average prices for the products that have been jointly produced. That is to say, the solution depicted at equilibrium determines a unique distribution of the *to-*

tal costs of production between the purchasers of the separate consumption components, as well as the indicated unique distribution of the marginal costs.

In the public-goods case, the jointness arises only because of the indivisibility or the nonexclusion in consumption. Resale of consumption units among separate demanders is impossible by definition. Therefore, the attainment of equilibrium determines uniquely only *marginal* prices confronting the several demanders. This equilibrium may be consistent with almost an infinite number of sharing schemes for the costs over inframarginal units. The prices need not be uniform either over varying quantities or as among separate persons. The average supply price for consumption units need not be equal to marginal price.

In orthodox price theory, the distinction between price discrimination among separate buyers and among separate quantities that may be purchased by a single buyer is noted, but seldom does it warrant particular attention. The reason for the underemphasis is simple; if resale of a good is possible without undue costs, neither type of discrimination can long exist. With public goods, however, resale is wholly impossible, either directly or indirectly. Differences in prices paid by separate persons have been demonstrated to emerge from ordinary motivations in trading. In this case, the distinction between price discrimination over quantity and price discrimination among persons becomes an important one. To clarify this point, consider the sale of a private service rather than a good, say nursing care. It is probable that a firm supplying this service will discriminate among separate buyers; this is standard practice in the pricing of most elements of medical care. Prices tend to be charged in some direct relationship to predicted income levels of the buyers. In addition, the firm may or may not discriminate in its charges to a single buyer over varying quantities of purchase. Its price per day of nursing care may be unchanged whether the single buyer takes one day's care, one week's, one month's or more. Or, perhaps more commonly, the firm may charge a lower price per day for longer periods; it may allow quantity discounts.

When goods and services are made available to a single buyer at differing prices for different quantities, the average price differs from the marginal price at each quantity. The buyer's choice will be distorted; he will be led by the conditions of the offer to purchase a total quantity either greater or less than that quantity which he would purchase at the same average price but with a uniform, and equal, marginal price. It is this phenomenon of possible price discrimination over quantity to a single buyer that requires discussion in some detail here. As the analysis above has indicated, discrimination in marginal prices among separate demanders or consumers of purely public goods emerges as the outcome of any efficiently organized trading process. In fact, as we have shown, the results in this respect are wholly analogous to Marshall's theory of joint supply; the use of the very term "price discrimination" in this instance seems itself to be questionable.

Beyond this acknowledged interpersonal differentiation in marginal prices, there remains open the question as to the relation between marginal prices and average prices confronted by the single buyer. What structure will emerge in this respect from the processes of trade? And what will be the effects of this structure on the equilibrium outcome? Methodologically, the analysis here is important. The repeated references to income-effect feedbacks in the earlier discussion may have seemed insignificant. But these feedbacks become of vital importance at this point. What we are confronted with is the appropriateness of such a notion as an individual marginal evaluation schedule or curve for a purely public good.

Individual Demand for a Public Good

Both in this chapter and in the one preceding we have introduced individual demand and/or marginal evaluation curves for a public good without careful definition. This gap must now be filled. The derivation of an individual demand curve or schedule for a private good is straightforward. The potential buyer is confronted, conceptually, with a set of all possible prices, and the maximum quantity that he stands ready to purchase at each price becomes a point in the schedule. In such a derivation, we assume that each offer embodies an equality between average and marginal price. That is to say, the individual demander is assumed to be faced with a series of supply schedules or curves, each of which allows him to vary quantity purchased without modifying average price. Without this critical assumption, no demand schedule for the individual could be derived, even for a purely private good. If, instead of uniform average-marginal prices, the buyer should be confronted with a set of separate "price offers" that contain varying relations between average and marginal price, no single-valued demand relationship between quantity demanded and either average or marginal price would exist. There would be no individual demand curve. Here the individual buyer would be in a position analogous to the monopolistic seller. In the latter case, there is no supply curve that may be derived. The monopolist faces, not a set of demand prices that are uniform over quantity (such as confront the competitive seller) but, instead, a set of demand schedules in the relevant market.

What has all of this to do with the derivation of an individual demand schedule for a purely public good? Can we not, at least conceptually, derive such a schedule in the same way that we derive the demand schedule for a private good? Can we not imagine that we confront the individual with a series of prices, uniform over the quantity range, and ask him what quantity he would prefer at each of these prices? Clearly such a procedure is possible, and we shall employ it in the following section. With public goods, however, this procedure is much more arbitrary than in the comparable private-goods model, and its usage may suggest apparent determinacy where none exists. In the world of private goods, most buyers of final products do face horizontal supply curves. The market economy operates to prevent the emergence of monopolistic quantity discounts or quantity premiums save in rare instances. For this reason an individual demand curve derived in the orthodox manner becomes a relevant tool of analysis. With public goods, by contrast, there are no institutions that prevent price discrimination over quantities, and such quantity differentials may well emerge from an open trading process. To analyze the demand for public goods, therefore, we need something akin to the orthodox demand curve but which possesses more general applicability.

There are three courses of action open. The first is the one already mentioned. We can quite arbitrarily assume that the individual is to be confronted with a set of uniform prices (tax-prices) for a public good. Given this device, a unique relationship between price and quantity demanded can be established. A second method has also been referred to in the simple exchange models of Chapter 2. Discrepancies between average and marginal prices over quantities exert an influence on the behavior of the buyer only because different offers extract from him different amounts of consumer's (taxpayer's) surplus. If such real-income effects can be assumed to be negligible or nonexistent, each marginal price must generate a uniquely preferred quantity, regardless of its relationship to average supply price. This procedure might be labeled the Marshallian escape route. In the standard indifference map construction, it amounts to assuming that the individual's indifference contours have the same slope along any vertical line, provided that we measure private goods (income) along the ordinate and public goods along the abscissa.

This neglect of income-effect feedbacks on individual marginal evaluation is helpful in presenting the elementary theory, but, like the initial method that involves marginal-price uniformity, it remains a device designed for didactic purpose. Income effects must be incorporated in any reasonably sophisticated analysis, and possible departures from marginal-price uniformity must also be allowed. This suggests resort to a third procedure, one that retains most of the pedagogic usefulness of the orthodox demand curve. This involves the introduction of the *marginal evaluation schedule* or *marginal evaluation curve*, which we have already used without careful definition or discussion.

The basic idea behind this construction is simple. The marginal evaluation schedule indicates the evaluations (in terms of a numeraire) placed on successive units of quantity as seriatim purchases are made by the individual. These evaluations will depend on the average price paid over inframarginal ranges. For every price offer, therefore, a different marginal evaluation schedule may be derived.

Geometrically, a marginal evaluation curve for an individual is derived by taking the slopes of successive indifference curves as these curves intersect a single opportunity curve over varying quantities of the public good. The curve embodies, therefore, the possible effects on the individual's choice behavior that are exerted by the sacrifice of real income over inframarginal ranges. The rate of required payment is determined by the specific shape of the opportunity curve over the relevant quantity range. The successive slopes of the opportunity curve provide a schedule of marginal prices, and this schedule can take any form. Marginal price may be equal to, greater than, or less than, average price through all or any part of the quantity range.

The deficiency of the marginal evaluation schedule or curve as an analytical tool lies in its dependence on the uniqueness of the opportunity curve or offer schedule. For each price offer represented by a single curve there can be derived a different marginal evaluation curve or schedule. This is illustrated in Figure 3.2(a)–(b). Assume that a person is faced with a standard

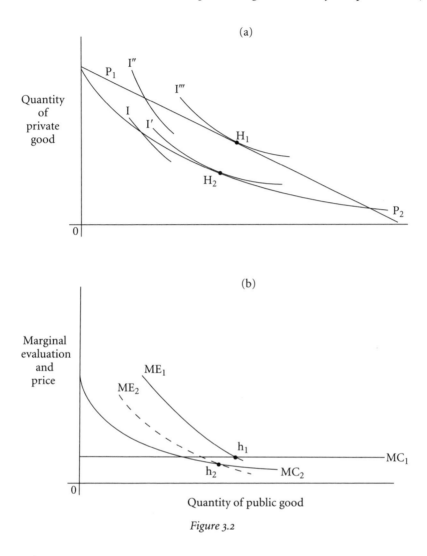

Figure 3.2

uniform price offer represented geometrically by the linear opportunity line, P_1, in Figure 3.2(a). Given this offer, we derive a marginal evaluation curve by tracing the slopes of the successive indifference curves as they cut this opportunity line. Such a curve is drawn in Figure 3.2(b) and is labeled, ME_1. Marginal cost or marginal supply price is simply the slope of P_1, which in this case is constant over quantity. The curve of marginal cost is shown as MC_1. Equilibrium is shown at H_1 and h_1 on the two parts of Figure 3.2.

Note that the marginal evaluation curve, ME_1, *does not* tell us anything at all about how much the person would purchase at any other supply price or price offer. It is not, therefore, analogous to the demand curve in this general sense. The construction does enable us, with facsimiles of the Marshallian tools, to depict the characteristics of the final equilibrium position for the individual. Only in this sense does the marginal evaluation construction resemble that of the orthodox demand curve in the absence of further qualifying assumptions.

If the individual whose choice is examined should be confronted with an alternative supply price offer or opportunity, a different marginal evaluation curve and a different marginal supply price must be derived. One such alternative offer is shown as curve P_2, in Figure 3.2(a). Here the buyer is faced with an opportunity to purchase the good at a quantity discount. Marginal price falls below average price throughout the quantity range. In the same way as before, we can construct a marginal evaluation curve by plotting the slopes of the successive indifference curves as they cut P_2. This curve is drawn as ME_2 in Figure 3.2(b). The marginal cost or marginal supply price curve now becomes MC_2. Equilibrium is again shown at H_2 and h_2. Note that the marginal evaluation curve cannot be employed "to locate" the equilibrium position, given changing offers or supply price. To use the curve in this fashion would involve circular reasoning. The construction does, however, present a picture of equilibrium, once attained.

Determinacy Restored by Marginal-Price Uniformity

The discussion in the preceding section may seem unduly tedious, but it is fundamental to an understanding of the theory of public goods. At equilibrium, the marginal rates of substitution between the public good and the numeraire private good, summed over all persons in the group, must equal the marginal cost of supplying the public good, again expressed in units of the numeraire. This statement of the necessary marginal conditions for equilibrium in a world that contains a public good is fully general, and holds without qualification. It is erroneous, however, to infer from this statement of the necessary marginal conditions that an external observer can locate or find the equilibrium supply of public goods by summing individual marginal evaluation curves or schedules and comparing these sums with observed marginal costs. In geometric terms, it is erroneous to sum vertically the separate individual marginal evaluation schedules and then to locate the equilibrium or optimal supply of the public good at the point where the aggregate curve cuts the curve of marginal cost.

This conclusion need not imply that we dispense with the simple Marshallian geometry. It does suggest that we handle the tools properly and with due caution. Does there exist a methodologically legitimate means of utilizing the familiar constructions to find equilibrium in the supply of public goods, given individuals' utility functions and the costs of the good to the community of persons? As is indicated above, in the general case where marginal-price uniformity cannot be assumed present and where income effects cannot be neglected, there is no such means. If used with proper caution, however, the arbitrary convention regarding marginal-price uniformity revitalizes the geometrical construction. Refer now to Figure 3.3. As before, assume that the public good is available to the community at constant marginal cost, indicated by the curve *MC*. We adopt the convention that tax-

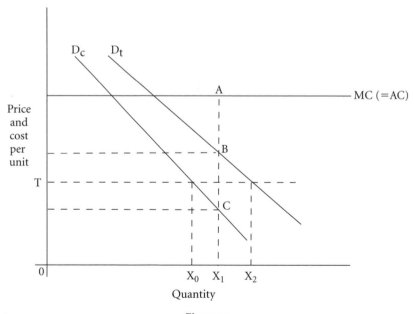

Figure 3.3

prices per unit of the good are to be uniform over various quantities for each person, although, of course, these need not be uniform as among separate persons. This step allows us to derive demand curves for the public good in the orthodox fashion. Conceptually, we simply confront each individual with the opportunity to "purchase" or to "vote for" a most preferred quantity at each price (marginal = average). These curves for Tizio and Caio are labeled D_t and D_c in Figure 3.3. (Note specifically that these are *not* marginal evaluation curves.) The information contained in these demand curves and the cost curve allows us to determine uniquely the efficient supply of the public good and the equilibrium set of marginal tax-prices that each person must confront. $0X_1$ represents this quantity, and BX and CX the equilibrium marginal-average tax-prices. The determinacy here is introduced through our assumption as to the uniformity in tax-price over quantity. This assumption or convention, which is admittedly an arbitrary even if a reasonable one, allows income effects to be included in the model, but it does so only by guaranteeing one particular division of the gains-from-trade that are secured in producing the public good.

This particular sharing scheme is directly analogous to that which ordinary trading processes generate in the private-goods world where resale possibilities exist. Since these do not exist, by definition, in the public-goods world, such a sharing scheme must be arbitrarily introduced or "constitutionally" agreed upon by all participants. Once accepted, and given a set of initial resource endowments, and given the utility and cost functions, equilibrium is uniquely determined.

The manner in which our two-person group could grope its way toward a final equilibrium adjustment under this convention of marginal-price uniformity can be shown readily. Suppose that the two traders initially agree that tax-prices for units of the public good to be confronted by each person are to remain uniform over quantities. Suppose further that each person recognizes the publicness of the good at the outset, but that no strategic behavior takes place. This latter assumption is useful in that we want to utilize the small-number model as an analogue for large-number situations where strictly strategic behavior may be absent. Tizio takes it upon himself to propose various sharing schemes, all within the price-uniformity convention. Initially, he proposes that each person should pay one-half of the marginal cost per unit of the public good, represented on Figure 3.3 by the tax-price $0T$. At this level,

Caio will agree to finance only a quantity, $0X_0$, whereas Tizio will desire to finance an amount, $0X_2$. Since the two persons must agree on a single quantity, the initial proposal fails and Tizio then makes an alternative proposal, increasing his own tax-price and, *pari passu,* reducing that confronting Caio. He will proceed to modify the offer in this fashion until Caio agrees on the same desired quantity that he himself prefers. And, as the construction indicates, only the amount, $0X_1$, fits this requirement under the price-uniformity constraint that we have imposed.

In utilizing this convention or assumption as a means of shoring up the usefulness of Marshallian geometry, we are implicitly selecting the final position on the Pareto welfare surface. Other positions of final equilibrium embodying different distributions of the taxpayers' surplus may be equally relevant in any given real-world situation, and no "efficiency" attributes characterize the arbitrary position that the convention produces. There is, nonetheless, something more than mere analytical convenience in the price-uniformity convention. Uniformity in tax-price over quantity is characteristic of any tax-sharing scheme that maintains constant share progressivity. Since many major revenue producers in real-world fiscal systems meet this requirement, the model warrants analytical distinction, provided that its limitations are kept in mind.

Bibliographical Appendix

The separate demanders of a purely public good must be charged different marginal prices if the necessary conditions for efficiency are attained. This has been recognized, with varying degrees of precision, by almost all contributors to the voluntary exchange theory of public finance from Sax down to the present day. The requirement is implicit in Wicksell's early treatise. It becomes quite explicit in Lindahl, and it is also stressed in Howard Bowen's early modern formulation ["The Interpretation of Voting in the Allocation of Resources," *Quarterly Journal of Economics,* LVIII (November 1943), 27–48]. It is contained in both Musgrave's and Samuelson's statements of the theory, but it is not emphasized. In his valuable survey paper, J. G. Head states the requirement for differential marginal prices concisely ["Public Goods and Public Policy," *Public Finance,* XVII (No. 3, 1962), 197–221]. Essentially the same problem arises in the theory of public-utility pricing under joint costs. An early and important statement was made by Donald H. Wallace ["Joint and Overhead Costs and Railway Rate Policy," *Quarterly Journal of Economics*, XLVIII (August 1934), 583–619]. Recent contributions have concentrated on peak-load adjustments and have stressed the necessity of differing marginal prices in separate periods; these include papers by H. S. Houthakker, Peter Steiner, Jack Hirschleifer, and Oliver Williamson [Houthakker, "Electricity Tariffs in Theory and Practice," *Economic Journal*, LXI (March 1951), 1–25; Steiner, "Peak Loads and Efficient Pricing," *Quarterly Journal of Economics*, LXXI (November 1957), 585–610; Hirschleifer, "Peak Loads and Efficient Pricing: Comment," *Quarterly Journal of Economics*, LXXII (August 1958), 451–62; Williamson, "Peak-Load Pricing and Optimal Capacity Under Indivisibility Constraints," *American Economic Review*, LVI (September 1966), 810–27].

In the monograph cited previously, Milton Z. Kafoglis noted the distinction between those external economies that arise from the act of producing a good or service for common consumption and those that arise from the act of consuming as such [*Welfare Economics and Subsidy Programs*, University of Florida Monographs in Social Science, No. 11, Summer 1961].

The joint-supply characteristic of public goods has been specifically treated, in general terms, by Carl Shoup ["Public Goods and Joint Production," *Rivista internazionale di scienze economiche e commerciali*, XII (1965), 254–64]. In the valuable survey paper cited in the preceding paragraph, Head has also developed this aspect of the theory. Geometrical models based on Marshallian joint-supply analysis were extended to apply to an impure public good in a paper by James M. Buchanan and Milton Z. Kafoglis ["A Note on Public Goods Supply," *American Economic Review*, LIII (June 1963), 403–14]. The distinction between units of production and units of consumption was discussed in my 1966 paper ["Joint Supply, Externality, and Optimality," *Economica*, XXXIII (November 1966), 404–15].

The difficulties raised by income-effect feedbacks on allocative outcomes in public-goods models were noted by Paul A. Samuelson in his two basic papers ["The Pure Theory of Public Expenditure," *Review of Economics and Statistics*, XXXVI (November 1954), 387–89; "Diagrammatic Exposition of a Theory of Public Expenditure," *Review of Economics and Statistics*, XXXVII (November 1955), 350–56]. The implications of this relationship were emphasized by Robert H. Strotz in his note ["Two Propositions Related to Public Goods," *Review of Economics and Statistics*, XL (November 1958), 329–31]. The importance of the feedback income effects on allocative solutions in the related peak-load pricing problem was the main point of my comment ["Peak Loads and Efficient Pricing: Comment," *Quarterly Journal of Economics*, LXXX (August 1966), 563–71]. André Gabor provided a more rigorous analysis of this application ["Further Comment," *Quarterly Journal of Economics*, LXXX (August 1966), 512–80].

The derivation of marginal evaluation curves was discussed by J. R. Hicks in an early paper ["The Four Consumer Surpluses," *Review of Economic Studies*, XI (1943), 31–42]. In a 1952 paper, I developed this construction in a particular application ["The Theory of Monopolistic Quantity Discounts," *Review of Economic Studies*, XX (1952–53), 199–208].

4. Pure and Impure Public Goods

We have come part of the way in generalizing the models of simple exchange with which the analysis commenced in Chapter 2. The restrictive assumptions as to the identity of our two traders in both tastes and in productive capacity have been abandoned. Income effects have been introduced into the analysis. In this chapter, we propose to drop another one of the initial assumptions, that which requires purity in the public good. For the present, we shall remain in the two-person world. The limitation to two goods at the production level will be retained, although the introduction of impurity leads necessarily to a third *consumption good*. We shall explore the process through which equilibrium is attained when one good is something less than wholly or purely collective in the strict sense.

By the orthodox definition a pure public good or service is *equally available* to all members of the relevant community. A single unit of the good, as produced, provides a multiplicity of consumption units, all of which are somehow identical. Once produced, it will not be efficient to exclude any person from the enjoyment (positive or negative) of its availability. To use the terminology preferred by R. A. Musgrave, the principle of exclusion characteristic of goods produced in the market breaks down here. Nonexclusion applies in the extreme or polar sense. Additional consumers may be added at zero marginal cost.

This definition is highly restrictive, and it is not surprising that the modern theory of public goods has been criticized on this basis. Strictly speaking, no good or service fits the extreme or polar definition in any genuinely descriptive sense. In real-world fiscal systems, those goods and services that are financed publicly always exhibit less than such pure publicness. The standard examples such as national defense come reasonably close to descriptive purity, but even here careful consideration normally dictates some relaxation of the strict polar assumption. It is evident that the whole theory would be severely limited if it were to stand or fall on the correspondence of this purity assumption with observations from the real world.

Fortunately the theory has a much wider base, and I shall demonstrate that it retains general validity independent of the descriptive characteristics of particular goods and services. In so doing, however, I shall also show that attempts to employ the classification as a tool in determining what goods and services should be organized collectively rather than privately must be abandoned, at least provisionally. The theory of public goods when properly interpreted becomes applicable to *any* good or service, quite independent of its physical attributes. The theory's relevance depends upon the institutional arrangements through which the political group organizes the supply of goods and services. In one sense, the approach here amounts to an inversion of the theory as conceived by some modern scholars. Instead of using the model to classify the appropriateness of alternative institutional arrangements, I shall demonstrate the model's usefulness and general validity with respect to all goods and services that happen, for any reason, to be organized and supplied publicly.

Private Goods as Public Goods

Initially, let us take a good that under normal circumstances we know to be purely private. A unit that is produced corresponds to a unit consumed by only one person, and neither its production nor its consumption generates, positively or negatively, relevant external or spillover effects on persons other than the direct consumer. If we can show that the theory of public goods properly interpreted can be made applicable even for this sort of good, then it should become clear that we can utilize the same tools for a good or service that falls anywhere along the whole indivisibility spectrum.

For simple illustrative purposes, think of such a good as bread. Under normal circumstances, a unit of this good, defined in physical units produced or consumed per unit time, can be transformed into only one consumption unit. That is to say, only one person can enjoy directly the benefits of a loaf of bread in a single time period. It is physically impossible for you and me to eat the same loaf of bread. Even here, however, we can analyze the attainment of trading equilibrium with the tools provided by the theory of pure public goods. The critical step is to define the good properly. Generically, "bread" is privately divisible among separate consumers, and we cannot apply the theory of indivisible goods to the demand and the supply of "bread" as so defined. We may, however, define the "good" that we propose to analyze in such a manner that it does embody the necessary indivisibility characteristics. To do so, all that is required is that we define our commodity in terms of *identifiable units*. In this example, define the good to be analyzed as "my bread." There will then be as many separate "my breads" as there are persons, all within the single generically defined commodity group "bread." But with this relatively simple definitional step, we can proceed to apply the theory without qualification.

Take one of these *n* goods, say, "your bread." Assume, for any reason, that the community of which you are a member has decided that this is to be supplied publicly. You are not allowed to produce, purchase or consume "your bread" until and unless you are able to secure the permission of other members of the group. Let us assume the existence of a Wicksellian unanimity rule for making community decisions. In this case, the characteristics of equilibrium are not difficult to define. Since the marginal evaluation of "your bread" is zero for all other persons and over all quantities, it will be unnecessary for you to engage in "trade" with them. Equilibrium is attained when your own marginal evaluation equals the marginal cost of production. This is, of course, the same equilibrium that the market process generates. Nevertheless, the identity of the standard theory of markets and the theory of public goods in this instance is worth emphasizing. Note that, using the latter, we can say that the summed marginal rates of substitution between the "public good" and some numeraire private good must equal marginal cost. This statement of the necessary marginal conditions of optimality holds without qualification. We are, in this example, merely adding a string of zeros to a single positive value in the summation process.

The Unit of Joint Supply

The necessity of treating each person's consumption good separately is, of course, dictated by the objective of utilizing the tools provided by the theory of public goods. Once we have demonstrated the possibility of such an extension, there need be no such analysis for a genuinely private good since, by definition, the standard theory of private-goods exchange applies. Our interest here is not with this theory but with extending the theoretical apparatus developed in application to purely public goods to cover "impure" goods, those neither purely private nor purely public. This raises the question as to whether the conditions for equilibrium can be derived in some fashion that will not require n separate statements, one for each person's identifiable units of possession.

Once again, it is useful to recall the theory of joint supply. This will allow us to introduce a simplification. The necessary condition for equilibrium is that the summed marginal evaluations of the consumption components must be equal to the marginal cost of the production unit. Apply this condition to the purely public good. The production unit, or unit of joint supply, provides or embodies n-consumption units, when n is the number of persons in the group. Since there is only one production unit, however, the analysis can be limited to this single unit dimension on the cost side. The same analysis may be extended readily to purely private goods, however, provided only that we make the *same* summation over persons on the cost side as we do on the demand side. The general condition necessary for optimality in all cases is that summed marginal evaluation equals summed marginal cost, with the units appropriately defined.

The Fixity of Proportions—Equal Shares

Marshall's theory of joint supply commences with the assumption that the final products or product components are in fixed proportions. If variability in proportions is allowed, additional conditions must be derived and the analysis becomes more complex. As we noted earlier, with a public good the assumption of pure publicness guarantees that different consumers have available to them equal shares. This begs the issue, however, and suggests a further examination into the precise meaning of the terms "equal shares" or "equal availability." What do we mean by saying that a publicly supplied good or service is "equally available" to all members of the community?

First of all, as already noted, this does not imply that the marginal evaluations placed on the good by the separate consumers are equal. In some of the literature of modern public-goods theory, equal availability seems to mean that each consumer has available for his use the *same quantity* of consumption units. This gets us nowhere, however, until we can clarify the meaning of the "same quantity." What does it suggest to say that Mr. *A* has the *same quantity* of public good or service *X* available to him as does Mr. *B*?

Let us once again take a simple illustration, fire protection. How do we go about measuring quantity of such a service? One procedure might be to define units of service flow in terms of the probability that destructive fire will damage property. If fire protection provided by the community to Mr. *A* is sufficient to insure that on any given day there is only a .0005 probability that his property will suffer fire damage in excess of $100, we can say that more protection is provided than if this probability should be .0007. This manner of defining the quantity of service flows utilizes *homogeneous-quality consumption units*. This is, of course, the standard way in which we measure quantities of privately supplied goods and services.

If this procedure is followed, however, the theory of public goods does not carry us very far, if indeed it carries us anywhere at all. There are, in reality, no purely public goods if equal availability is measured in such terms as these. At this point, it is useful to recall the earlier apparent digression where the theory of public goods was extended to apply to the purely private good, "your bread." We said that the commodity, "your bread," was equally available to all members of the community. In that formulation, we could not have possibly been defining equal availability in terms of similar quantities of homogeneous-quality consumption units. We must have been applying some measurement procedure different from that which economists apply to fully divisible private goods and services.

Again the theory of joint supply is helpful. To the extent that a good or service, as produced, satisfies more than one demand, we can measure quantity, not in homogeneous-quality consumption units, but in *production units*. And there is nothing inherent in the jointness of supply, *per se*, which suggests that different demanders need enjoy or have available to them homogeneous-quality units for final consumption. This point is, of course, made evident in Marshallian joint supply, where final consumption components may be demonstrably different in some physically descriptive sense (meat and hides). The point is less apparent, but equally valid, with reference to publicly supplied goods and services. In our fire protection example, suppose that a fire station is physically located nearer to Mr. *A*'s residence than to Mr. *B*'s. In terms of homogeneous-quality final consumption, these two persons do not enjoy the same quantity of fire protection. However, the services of the fire station, given its physical location, are equally available to both *A* and *B*, and, as joint consumers, they may be said to enjoy the same quantity of the public good, fire protection, so long as the latter is defined strictly in *production or supply units.*

The differentiation in the physical quality and in the quantity of consumption goods and services supplied to separate persons will, of course, be reflected in the different marginal evaluations placed on the jointly supplied inputs. Hence, in our illustration, even if *A* and *B* should have identical utility functions and identical incomes, *B* will place a lower marginal evaluation on the publicly supplied service of fire protection for the simple reason that, translated into units relevant for his own consumption, he enjoys a lower-quality and smaller-quantity product. It is because of this translation of differential service flows into differential marginal evaluations that difficulties arise in any attempt to separate genuine differences in tastes from differences in physical service flows.

The analysis here suggests that the theory of public goods can be meaningfully discussed only when the units are defined as "those which are jointly supplied" and when "equal availability" and, less correctly, "equal consumption" refer only to jointly supplied production units or inputs, which may and normally will embody widely divergent final consumption units, measured by ordinary quality and quantity standards. Interpreted in this way, the theory becomes very general.

If a good or service is supplied jointly to several demanders or consumers, the question arises whether the "mix" among the separate components is fixed or variable. In Marshall's example, the unit of production (the steer, the physical characteristics of which were initially assumed to be invariant) determined uniquely the meat and hides content in each jointly supplied bundle. In our own illustration, the *fixed location* of the fire station determines uniquely the relative quality-quantity of the services received by *A* and by *B*. For any publicly supplied good or service, the availability of which is open to all members of a group, the proportions in the mix are set by the locational-technological characteristics of the supplied units.[2] Once these are set, the analogue to the Marshallian fixed-proportion model is complete.

In the sense noted here, public goods or services will normally be multidimensional. Not only must the location of the fire station in the municipality be fixed, but all the other characteristics of the public service must also be specified to the extent that these influence in any way the quality-quantity of final consumption components received by different demanders-users. To simplify, we may use "location" as a surrogate for all such characteristics. In our fire station illustration, this amounts to assuming that the sole characteristic of the fire station that influences the relative quality-quantity of fire protection received by A and B is its location. It is evident, of course, that many such problems of dimensionality arise in the provision of almost any public good or service. A police force better trained to break up street riots than to track down safecrackers will nevertheless be equally available to citizens who have plate glass windows in main streets and to citizens who keep large cash sums in safes. But the relative amount of protection actually received by each group will depend on the technical mix of this composite force, this being the unit of joint supply in the appropriate jurisdiction. Once the technical characteristics of this unit are set, the physical consumption flows to the different demanders are combined in fixed proportions and the analogy with Marshall's fixity in proportions is direct. If these characteristics are assumed to be determined by noneconomic, engineering considerations that are divorced from the respective preferences of the demanders, the theory of public goods can be applied without difficulty and emendation. No

2. This statement suggests one important aspect of public-goods supply that may have been overlooked by some scholars. The theory of public goods can be applied even in those cases where congestion arises in the usage of a public facility. A road, street or highway provides the best illustration of this point. The facility, once constructed, is made equally available to all users, and the theory of public goods can be used to determine, conceptually, the appropriate extension in the capacity of the facility. Each facility embodies, however, a certain congestion probability as one of its physical dimensions, and this will be taken into account in the individual marginal evaluations. For example, an individual will place a different marginal evaluation on a toll-free, congested thoroughfare than on a toll-charging, noncongested throughway of the same physical attributes. Even in the toll-charging case, however, the facility is equally available to all potential users.

problem of determining the optimal mix among components in the jointly supplied unit need arise.

The Component Mix—the Technology of Public Goods

As the illustrative examples make clear, in ordinary cases of public-goods supply no such noneconomic considerations are paramount. The components in the appropriate units of joint supply can normally be varied within rather wide limits. Even if this should not prove possible in each instance, the theory should be generalized if at all possible to allow for such variability. It should be possible to lay down necessary conditions for optimality in the mix. The structure will remain seriously incomplete unless we can isolate, at least conceptually, the forces that make for distinct variations in the mix among the consumption components in a jointly supplied public good. Under what conditions should the fire station be located near *A* rather than *B*? Under what conditions should the police force be trained primarily to break up street riots rather than to locate burglars? We need to examine the conditions for equilibrium or optimality in the component mix in addition to the more familiar conditions for equilibrium or optimality in the quantity of the production units that are to be supplied.

Note that this problem arises only with publicly supported goods and services that are impure. They must be neither wholly private, in the sense of no spillover benefits or harms arising from their production or consumption, nor wholly public, in the sense of strictly equal consumption of homogeneous-quality units of good or service. In the first case, even if the supply should be publicly organized, there is no question of defining the optimal mix since each demander's preferences can be satisfied independently and separately. In the second case, there will be no interpersonal quality-quantity variability by definition. The interesting cases are those falling between these polar limits. And here interpersonal and intergroup variability can readily be incorporated into the production process, even within the overall technological constraints that dictate the relative efficiency of joint supply. In illustrative terms, the fire station can readily be located at any one of several places, each one of which embodies a different mix among consumption components, despite the fact that, wherever located, within wide limits, *A* and *B* will still find it relatively more efficient to secure their fire protection services jointly rather than separately.

Equilibrium in the Mix

Let us now return to our simple Tizio-Caio model to discuss this problem concerning optimality in the mix, one that has not been adequately developed in the modern literature. In the model of simple exchange, introduced first in Chapter 2, we assumed that one of the two goods was purely public in the strictest definitional sense. We presumed, without really raising the issue for serious critical scrutiny, that each of the two consumers enjoyed equal quantities of homogeneous consumption units. That is to say, we assumed that the killing of one mosquito, whenever or wherever, provided an equal quality service flow to Tizio and to Caio. As the discussion in the preceding sections suggests, this highly restrictive feature of the model must now be modified. We propose to make the two consumption components enjoyed by Tizio and Caio into two conceptually distinct goods. Both Tizio and Caio place positive valuation on mosquito repelling services, but let us assume that the two men sleep at different locations. Therefore, the location of the public good or service can modify the mix between the two components.

If it should be technologically necessary to release mosquito repellent at only one place, the earlier analysis would not be affected in any way and no additional conditions need be derived. The fact that, in some descriptive sense, the final consumption components should amount to quite different goods would in this case be wholly irrelevant to the analytics. As we have suggested this seems an overly restrictive model, and we want to examine one in which the mix is variable. Assume that although Tizio and Caio will always find it relatively efficient to control mosquitoes jointly rather than separately, variations are possible in this production-supply process that within wide limits will favor one or the other of the two components. We want to examine the process through which Tizio and Caio attain some equilibrium supply of mosquito repellent, but, also, we want to examine the process through which they attain some equilibrium mix among consumption components that characterize this public good. How much repellent or repellent services should be produced, and where should this activity take place?

The Mix of a Pure Public Good: The Limiting Case of One-for-One Correspondence Among Consumption Components

The problem of determining the optimal mix among consumption components in a jointly supplied production unit when this mix is variable may be discussed with the geometrical constructions to be introduced in this section. It will be helpful to present this construction first under the assumption that the mix is completely invariant in an extreme or limiting case where there is a one-for-one correspondence among the separate consumption components. Let us say that technological characteristics are such that every person receives equal quantities of homogeneous-quality consumption units from each unit of public good that is produced.

In Figure 4.1, this case becomes easy to diagram. The final consumption components enjoyed by the two demanders, Tizio and Caio, are measured along the abscissa and ordinate, respectively. Production can take place only along the 45° line as shown. A unit of production becomes two units of consumption. A unit of final consumption supplied to one person automatically

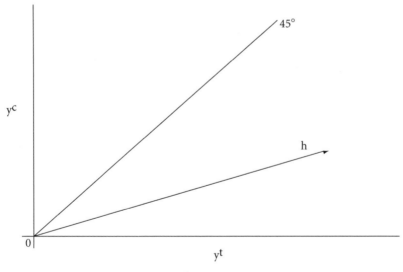

Figure 4.1

insures that a unit is also supplied at the same time to the remaining consumer, or consumers, in the group. It becomes impossible, by definition, to produce a unit of y^t, the consumption component enjoyed by Tizio, without at the same time, and jointly, producing precisely one unit of y^c, the consumption component enjoyed by Caio. As the geometrical construction suggests, the only problem in this highly restricted model is one of determining the optimal extension of production along the 45° ray. No problem of determining the optimal or equilibrium mix arises here.

The construction is useful, even in such a highly restricted model, in indicating that the separate consumption components need not be physically or descriptively identical if consumption units are defined only in terms of the contents of the production units. Tizio may be receiving mosquito repellent and Caio tick repellent, to vary our illustration, while the production of insect repellent qualifies as that of the pure public good. All that is required here is that there be a one-for-one correspondence among the separate consumption components in the mix and that this mix be invariant. In terms of *production units,* all demanders are receiving or enjoying identical goods here. *Consumption units* enjoyed by the separate parties may be (although they need not be) quite different one from the other in a descriptive sense.

The Mix of a Pure Public Good: Fixed Proportions

There need not exist such a one-for-one correspondence among separate consumption components in all public goods, even in those which can be classified as "purely public" in some more general sense. If units of final consumption enjoyed by each demander are measured *independently* in some physical dimension the quantities received by each person need not match up one-for-one. Consider once again fire protection, received by Tizio and Caio from a fixed-location fire station that is not equidistant from their properties. Each expansion in the production of the gross commodity, fire protection, at this fixed location will provide additional protection to both persons. But this need not be one-for-one. If, for instance, the fire house is nearer to Tizio than to Caio, an additional set of hoses on the fire engine may add three times the quantity of protection to Tizio that it adds to Caio. Production here can take place only along the ray h on Figure 4.1, indicating a three-for-one, not a one-for-one ratio. Note that here, as before, the pure public good is equally available to both demanders in *production unit* terms.

It would, of course, always be possible to redefine quantity units of consumption in such a way as to restore the one-for-one correspondence. If each consumption unit is measured in units of quantity contained in each *unit of production*, then each person enjoys equal quantities, by construction. It seems probable that this procedure has been implicit in much of the discussion of the theory, which has not included discussion of the mix among components. This convention of redefining quantity units may be helpful in certain cases, but here it obscures the very problem that we seek to examine. Once it is fully recognized that, in terms of final consumption units enjoyed, equal availability means little or nothing, the question that arises concerns the possibility of varying the component mix.

The Mix Under Variability of Proportions

Any general model must allow for variability in the mix among separate consumption components of jointly supplied goods and services, whether or not these be publicly provided. The two preceding models, in which such variability is not allowed, serve only to emphasize the restrictiveness of the standard public-goods assumption. It is difficult to think of practical public-goods examples where variability, within some limits, is not feasible. Mosquito repellent can be released in many parts of the island; fire stations can be located in many places; police forces can be variously trained.

Once this sort of variability is allowed, however, the necessary conditions for optimality in this mix must be determined in addition to the necessary conditions for optimality in the extension of production of the public good or service. Public-goods theory, as developed over the last quarter-century, has been almost exclusively devoted to the second of these problems, as has been almost all of the discussion in Chapters 2 and 3 above.

The analysis for the two-person, two-component model can be presented geometrically. In Figure 4.2, as in Figure 4.1, the two consumption components are measured along the axes. One simplifying assumption is necessary at the outset. The total cost function for each component, when and if *separate* production takes place, is linear. This assumption insures that if there are no efficiencies in joint production, iso-cost curves will also be linear. The

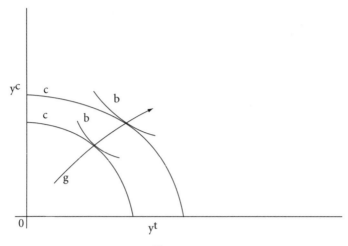

Figure 4.2

impure public good that we want to analyze does, however, embody net efficiency in joint production of the two components. This efficiency is indicated by the convexity of the iso-cost curves, the *c* curves in Figure 4.2.

As these curves are drawn, note that individual behavior under independent production would not generate external economies. If each person
should be required to produce his consumption component separately for
his own use, it will be efficient for him to exclude the other person from the
enjoyment of any spillover benefits. An alternative construction could be introduced (in which the *c* curves exhibit positive slopes over some ranges, as
do those in Figure 4.4) which would incorporate observed external economies under wholly independent behavior. In this construction, joint production would remain efficient, but, also, nonexclusion would characterize
privately organized supply. For analytical purposes at this point, either of
these two constructions is suitable. All that we require is that the joint supply
of the two components be relatively more efficient than separate supply.

The iso-cost curves are derived by mapping onto the surface of Figure 4.2
the contour lines from the appropriate total cost surface. Cost is measured
in units of some numeraire private good, along an axis extended outward
from the surface of the figure.[3] These iso-cost contours indicate the marginal

3. Under the restricted assumption of linearity in the two cost functions under sepa-

rate of substitution between the two consumption components on the production side. Before the necessary conditions for optimality in the mix between components can be derived, we need to determine, for each level of production, the rates at which these components may be substituted, one for the other, in the combined evaluation of the two traders. To simplify the presentation here, we have assumed that Tizio and Caio are interested solely in the consumption services that they receive directly. That is to say, neither person places a value on consumption flows to the other person. For a single person, therefore, indifference contours mapped onto Figure 4.2 would take the form of a series of parallel lines vertical to his own service flow axis. We are interested, however, in the joint or combined evaluation that the two men place on the two components in the mix. To secure a total benefit or total evaluation surface it is necessary to add the two individual benefit or evaluation surfaces in the private-goods or numeraire dimension. Once this step is taken, we can draw contour lines which can be mapped onto Figure 4.2 as iso-benefit or iso-evaluation curves. One such set is shown as the *b* curves. So long as diminishing marginal rates of substitution between the consumption component and money hold for each person, the iso-benefit curves must exhibit the convexity properties shown by the *b* curves.

The tangency between an iso-outlay and an iso-benefit curve is a necessary marginal condition for optimality in the mix of the two components at each level of production. The path along which production should proceed is indicated, therefore, by the locus of such tangency points, the ray labeled *g* in Figure 4.2. In this construction, we have again neglected income-effect feedbacks. Full incorporation of these would have made it impossible to derive iso-evaluation contours independent of the cost-sharing arrangements over inframarginal ranges, and these effects might also have modified the shape of the optimal-mix path over these ranges.

Once the ray or path of optimal mix among separate components in the jointly supplied unit of production is determined, there remains only the de-

---

rate production, the convexity of the iso-cost contours implies net efficiency in joint production. If, however, this linearity assumption is dropped, convex iso-cost contours may exist even where there is no jointness advantage. For this more general model, a redefinition of quantity units in terms of dollars of cost is required to convert the independent-production cost functions into effectively linear form. Once this step is taken, the analysis proceeds as it does in the simpler model.

termination of the rate of production along this ray or path. The solution here is quite straightforward, and it is the familiar one. It is represented by taking the derivative of the cost function along this optimal-mix path and equating it with the derivative for the total benefit function taken along the same path. Figure 4.3, which has a familiar look about it to economists, depicts this solution geometrically. Measured along the abscissa are units of production along the defined path. Measured along the ordinate are units of the private or numeraire good. The necessary conditions for optimal extension in production are satisfied when the slopes of the two functions are equal, again recalling the required neglect of income-effect feedbacks for this simplified construction here.

Note that this statement of the necessary marginal conditions is equivalent to that presented earlier in the simpler models. At the margin, a unit of production embodies two component "goods." In one sense, therefore, the marginal cost of supplying this combination represents the summed marginal costs of the two components. On the other side of the equation, the marginal benefits placed on the two components must equal the summation of the evaluations of the two demanders.

With this extension of the basic theory to the impure good which embodies widely varying proportions of the several components, but which is still characterized by efficiencies in joint supply, the analysis moves significantly toward generality. Although the construction becomes complex, the analysis is not modified in its essentials when we allow the separate demanders to place positive or negative evaluations on components in the mix other than the service flows which they receive directly. The owner of the plate glass window who is fearful of street riots can be allowed to place some value on the tracking down of safecrackers in the neighborhood, the prime interest of his neighbor. The characteristics of equilibrium are not modified. Both the purely public good and the purely private good become special cases of the more general theory that emerges here.

As we have noted, the separate demanders may value wholly different or quite similar components in the unit of jointly supplied good. For many public services, national parks for example, we normally think of separate persons enjoying similar physical facilities. Nevertheless, even such services as this can be best interpreted as embodying separate components. Where should a new park be constructed, and which existing ones should be ex-

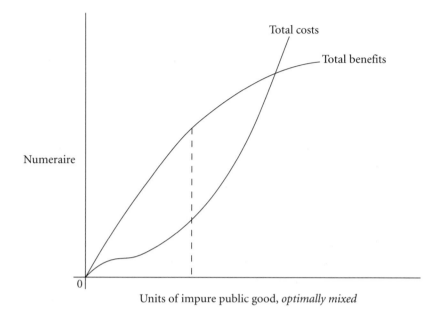

Figure 4.3

tended? The decision on such matters, insofar as efficiency criteria dictate, is precisely equivalent to that of determining the optimal mix among components. A decision to expand park facilities in Nevada rather than in West Virginia is a choice of a mix that includes a relatively smaller proportion of consumption units benefiting an easterner, and a relatively larger proportion of the units benefiting a westerner.

External Economies *in Consumption:* "Publicness" Without Orthodox Economies of Joint Supply

The phenomenon of joint supply has been the central feature of all public goods and services in the analysis developed to this point. The bases upon which individuals are motivated to organize the joint supply of any particular good or service has not been explored in detail, but implicit in the above discussion and in much of the standard literature is the assumption that technical characteristics inherent in the production process serve to make common sharing relatively efficient. The external economies arise in production, not consumption. Consider the classic examples. Why do the separate fishermen on the island refrain from building separate lighthouses? The act of producing a single lighthouse provides spillover or external benefits to all fishermen. Externally benefited parties care not at all whether or not the producer himself *consumes* the services that he produces. We propose to consider in this section the quite different model in which the external economies arise from the *act of consuming*. In this model, there need be no external economies from production in the orthodox sense, hence, no jointness efficiencies. With some stretching of the analysis, this model can be incorporated into the general public-goods model already developed.

Earlier in this chapter, the possible extension of the basic analytical model to purely private goods and services was examined, primarily for purposes of illustrating the generality of the tools. This discussion was then followed by showing how "impure" public goods may be brought into the analysis. Impurity or imperfect publicness in this respect was defined, however, as any departure from the availability of "equal quantities of homogeneous-quality consumption units" to all customers. Despite the presence of such impurities, the public-goods model was shown to hold so long as joint supply collectively or cooperatively organized is present.

We now want to assume away all jointness in supply, at least in this standard sense. We want to examine those instances where the external economies that may be present arise solely from the act of consumption. There is here, by definition, no spillover from production as such.

Consider a modified Tizio-Caio example. Through some daily expenditure of effort in digging out a special root and eating it, a person can make himself temporarily immune from a highly communicable disease. What form do the externalities take in this example? Tizio is not affected by Caio's *production* of the immunizing agent; there are no economies of joint production by definition. Tizio is, however, affected by, and hence interested in, Caio's *consumption* of the immunizing agent since Caio's immunity protects Tizio also and *vice versa*. Only in *consumption* is a "public good" produced.

A familiar real-world example that closely approximates this case arises in educational services. There are few, if any, necessary economies of joint supply on a scale sufficiently large to warrant consideration of collective organization. It is widely acknowledged, however, that important external economies or spillovers are generated in the act of consuming educational services. As a member of the political community, say a municipality, you are interested in the utilization or consumption of educational services by the child that lives in that community.

The extension of our basic theory to cover this case is not difficult. Here we resort to the approach already suggested when we treated any purely private good as a public good. *Each person's consumption or utilization of the service* must be considered separately, as an independent public good. You, as a member of the community, are interested here in n separate public goods, *each one* representing the educational services actually consumed by a single child in the same jurisdiction. For each of these n goods or services, joint supply in the orthodox fashion holds, and the necessary condition for full equilibrium may be derived as before. The marginal rates of substitution summed over all individuals in the group must be equal to the marginal cost of producing the service. When we discussed treating a purely private good as public, the procedure amounted to adding a series of zeroes to a single positive value. In the present case, where the external economies arise in consumption, we are confronted with an impure or in-between situation. Normally, the actual consumer of the services will place some differentially higher value on this consumption than his fellows. Such goods and services tend to exhibit considerable divisibility. In the case of educational services, a significantly higher evaluation will be placed on the services by the direct beneficiary, the family of the child who consumes. To this higher evaluation will normally be added, not a string of zeroes, and not a string of equal values, but a whole series of lower but still positive values.

Note that through this device of considering each person's consumption as a separate public service, we have converted the model into one where joint supply necessarily applies. Inherent in the education of the single child in the community is the joint supply of "this child's education" to all other members of the relevant group. The demands of all members are jointly met in the consumption of education by the single child. The analytical model developed earlier for other cases of impure public goods now holds without qualification. The problem of determining the optimal mix now becomes one of locating the quality standards that should characterize the educational services to be supplied to the particular child.

For simplicity in illustrating this point, let us resort to a two-person model again, with some variations, and remaining within the educational services illustration. Let us take Family Brown as our direct consumer. It has one child of school age, Charlie Brown, and the family, as a decision unit, is directly interested in Charlie's consumption of educational services. The rest of the community we treat here as a single person, called *ROC*, and this unit is also interested in the consumption of education by Charlie Brown. In Figure 4.4, we illustrate the problem as before by indicating possible variations in the mix among separate components.

We must define the units along the two axes in Figure 4.4 with some care. Along the horizontal axis, we measure physical service flows to the direct beneficiary of the child's utilization of educational facilities: in our case, Family Brown. Along the vertical axis, we measure physical service flows to the spillover beneficiaries stemming from the same utilization of educational facilities by the same child. Conceptually, these service flows are objectively computable. For purposes of analysis here, we may consider them to be measured in terms of reduced probabilities that the child will, when he becomes an adult, impose direct costs on the beneficiary. Such costs might take any of several forms: criminal, delinquent or antisocial behavior; substandard contribution to collectively organized activities; corrupt or suspect behavior in political process. The point to be emphasized is that the consumption of education by a single child generates some such physical flow of services both to the direct beneficiaries and to spillover beneficiaries. These physical flows

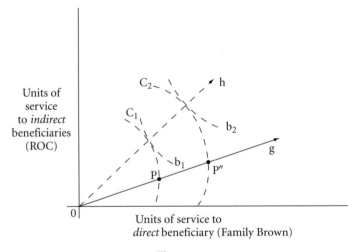

Figure 4.4

are measured on the axes of Figure 4.4. They must be kept conceptually distinct from individuals' *evaluations* placed on these flows. At this point, we are not directly concerned with the values, positive or negative, that direct or indirect beneficiaries may place on such service flows. Nor are we concerned here with problems of measuring such physical service flows in any empirical sense. Errors in estimation may, of course, cause individuals to place negative evaluations on service flows that objectively generate positive values. And, contrariwise, individuals may place positive evaluations on wholly imaginary flows of services.

As suggested, the behavior of direct beneficiaries in generating the consumption of educational facilities by a single child will normally provide some flow of services to other members of the community. Nonexclusion tends to be characteristic of such externalities. The privately generated behavior of the direct beneficiary, the family of the child who is being educated, may be depicted by its shift along the path *g* in Figure 4.4. As our earlier analysis of the public-goods mix suggested, if there is only one sort of education that can be consumed or utilized by the child, this path is unique. The incorporation of the interests of spillover beneficiaries, through some collectivization process, will serve only to shift the position of equilibrium outwards along the path *g*, say, from *P* to *P''*.

It seems obvious from the example here, however, that such "fixity in proportions" is not likely to occur. There are many variables in the education mix, and the "bundle" of facilities actually utilized by the child may vary within rather wide limits. It also seems reasonable that some of this variability can be related rather directly to the relationships between direct and indirect beneficiary service flows, the units measured along the axes in Figure 4.4. The education bundle can surely be modified to shift somewhat the proportions between the two categories of service flows. Own-family benefits may stem primarily from educational inputs that generate higher income expectations for the child, while spillover benefits may stem primarily from educational inputs that generate higher "cultural or citizenship" expectations. As surrogates for these two variables, we may think of vocational or professional versus general or classical education.

If such variability is possible, the optimal mix among components will be determined in the same manner that we have presented with respect to the more orthodox impure public good. Some generalizations may, however, be made here, suggesting that the analysis is not wholly without relevance or applicability to real-world problems. Consider the problem of determining the necessary conditions for optimality in the education of a single poor child as compared with the same conditions in the education of a single rich child. Presumably, the evaluation placed on the direct service flows to the own-family will be less in the former case than in the latter, hence the proportion of costs borne by the ROC will be greater. This suggests that, optimally, the education of the relatively poor child, or the child from poor parents, should contain a larger element of general material than that of the relatively rich child. Such generalizations from the analysis must, of course, be made with great care and with many qualifications. The direction of emphasis in variability may not be that which has been suggested here at all; also, efficiency considerations alone may not be of decisive importance. The implication is only that, if properly developed, the conceptual analysis here can lead to certain limited real-world predictions.

It must again be emphasized that, in treating of external economies that arise in the activity of consuming itself, each person's or family's activity must be considered as a separate public service in order to bring the analysis within the orthodox framework. One cannot combine the *n* separate "goods" into "education of all children" and employ the standard analysis. If this mistake is made, basic misunderstanding of this whole category is likely to arise. When we try to consider several persons' consumption or utilization of services simultaneously, we are really combining several separate externality relationships, with many resulting difficulties.

This analysis has important implications for the institutional arrangements of such consumption activities. What the analysis, along with the example, suggests is that the attainment of full equilibrium may involve participation of the whole membership of the community in financing the consumption activity of the single person, in the extreme cases, each person in the group, taken separately. What the analysis does not suggest is that the consumption activities of all persons, in our example, for all children, be jointly organized and supplied. Economies in the joint production of services for several persons may arise, of course. But such production economies are over and above, and quite different from, those consumption externalities that we have considered here. It is the latter which provide the basic motivation for potential collective-cooperative organization. Institutionally, the provision of facilities allowing the relevant consumption activity may be privately organized. Education may be supplied by private firms if this should prove the most efficient arrangement. The rest of the community may join with the direct beneficiary, the family, in purchasing privately supplied educational facilities. Equilibrium may well be attained most efficiently through ordinary competitive organization of the actual facilities, provided only that the community act somehow as a partner in the purchasing process. The incentive for cooperative action in such cases stems from the spillover benefits of consumption as such.

This case may again be contrasted with the orthodox public-good case when the spillovers or externalities arise from jointness and nonexcludability on the production side. Contrast education and police protection in this respect. You join forces with your neighbors in the municipality to finance education because you secure some benefit, for which you are willing to pay, from the consumption of services by your neighbor's child. You are willing to join forces with these same neighbors to produce, directly or indirectly, police protection (for both yourself and your neighbor) not because you are specifically interested in their own lives and property being protected, but because through joint action you can secure protection of your own life and property more efficiently. To bring the first case into the strict confines of the model developed to apply to the second case, which is basically the model for joint supply, we have shown that it is necessary to consider each person's separate consumption as an independent good. Because there is required here the organization of n separate goods, there is no apparent argument for monolithic supply. The direct implication for institutional structures is clear; with production externalities there is a particular efficiency reason for considering publicly managed or controlled supply of service facilities. With consumption externalities, the type of organization should be determined strictly by more orthodox efficiency criteria. The argument for "public schools" (as opposed to "public financing of education") must rest on a different footing from the argument for "public police protection."

A Formal Summary

We may summarize the extensions of the analysis introduced in this chapter by reference to the algebraic statements for equilibrium that were first presented in Chapter 2. Let us return to the Tizio-Caio model employed in that chapter for simplicity in exposition. Following the statements of conditions (9) and (10) in that chapter, we said: ". . . the conditions are fully general for two-person, two-good exchange, and these same statements encompass any degree of externality or publicness in x_2." If this earlier proposition holds, it should now be possible to summarize the analysis of Chapter 4 adequately through resort to these very general conditions for public-goods equilibrium. Conditions (9) and (10) are reproduced below for convenience. Recall that the superscripts refer to individuals; x_1 is the private good, x_2 the public good.

$$\frac{u^t x_2^c}{u^t x_1^t} = (-)\left[\frac{u^c x_2^c}{u^c x_1^c} - \frac{f^c x_2^c}{f^c x_1^c}\right]; \tag{9}$$

$$\frac{u^c x_2^t}{u^c x_1^c} = (-)\left[\frac{u^t x_2^t}{u^t x_1^t} - \frac{f^t x_2^t}{f^t x_1^t}\right]. \tag{10}$$

The u's represent partial derivatives of the utility functions, the f's partial derivatives of the cost functions facing the two persons. In more familiar terminology, the left-hand side of (9) represents Tizio's marginal evaluation of Caio's activity of producing the good, x_2, for his (Caio's) own consumption. The first term in the bracket represents Caio's own marginal evaluation of this same activity, while the second term represents his marginal cost. Under fully independent behavior, the bracketed terms sum to zero. The terms in (10) are similarly explained, with only the position of the two persons reversed.

Let us now consider four possible cases: (1) the pure private good, (2) the pure public good, (3) the impure public good characterized by indivisibilities, (4) the good that exhibits external economies in consumption but not in production.

The first case is straightforward and need not be examined in detail. Tizio will place no marginal evaluation on the production-consumption of x_2 by Caio, and Caio will not positively value similar activity by Tizio. The left-hand terms in both (9) and (10) become zero, and the conditions reduce to the familiar statements for equilibrium under wholly private adjustment.

The second case is also simple. Here we may take the first term out of the bracket and shift it to the left-hand side of the equation, producing the more familiar summation of marginal evaluations over the two individuals which is then equated to the marginal cost of supplying the good. In this case, we may drop either one of the two equations, (9) or (10), since they make identical statements. Each person's evaluation of the production-consumption activity of the other is fully equivalent to his evaluation of his own activity.

The third case is somewhat more difficult. Here the same quantities of homogeneous-quality consumption units are not available to both demanders, so that, even on the assumption of identical tastes, the evaluation that Tizio places on his own activity differs from that which he places on Caio's activity. The same relationship holds for Caio. Note that this case covers both the fixed proportion and the variable proportion good, since the conditions (9) and (10) do not relate to the definition of optimality in the component mix. Because the externalities here arise solely from production, from the relative efficiency of joint supply, either (9) or (10) may be dropped since production will tend to take place at only one "location." This case is different from the second, however, in that (9) and (10) will no longer be identical. Here either technological considerations will determine the precise location of x_2 or, more generally, the optimal mix will be determined by a consideration of both evaluation and cost factors. Before (9) or (10) is satisfied, these subsidiary conditions defining optimality in the component mix must be fulfilled.

In the fourth case, it is impossible to drop one of the two statements. Here the externalities arise not from production or joint-supply indivisibilities but from consumption activity, as such. Two separate collective or public goods must be considered, x_2^t and x_2^c, the first being the consumption of x_2 by Tizio, the second being the consumption of x_2 by Caio. For each of these two quite separate goods, the familiar public-goods conditions hold, and for each, the subsidiary conditions as to optimal mix must also be added. In this case, conditions (9) and (10) say quite different things, the one relating to one public good, the other to another.

Bibliographical Appendix

The initial criticisms of Samuelson's formulation of the theory of public goods were largely based on the limited applicability of the polar model [see Julius Margolis, "A Comment on the Pure Theory of Public Expenditure,"

Review of Economics and Statistics, XXXVII (November 1955), 347–49; G. Colm, "Comments on Samuelson's Theory of Public Finance," *Review of Economics and Statistics,* XXXVIII (November 1956), 408–12]. In his treatise, R. A. Musgrave recognizes the limitation of the full-exclusion model. This recognition was, perhaps, instrumental in his development of the category of "merit goods" [*The Theory of Public Finance* (New York: McGraw-Hill, 1959), Ch. 1]. This Musgrave category has been carefully examined by J. G. Head ["On Merit Goods," *Finanzarchiv* 25 (March 1966), 1–29]. In his 1966 paper, Musgrave analyzed several cases ["Provision for Social Goods" (Mimeographed, September 1966)]. In his second and third papers, and also in his later comment, Paul A. Samuelson responded to the criticisms concerning the polarity of his model ["Diagrammatic Exposition of a Theory of Public Expenditure," *Review of Economics and Statistics,* XXXVII (November 1955), 350–56; "Aspects of Public Expenditure Theories," *Review of Economics and Statistics,* XL (November 1958), 332–38; "Public Goods and Subscription TV: Correction of the Record," *Journal of Law and Economics,* VII (October 1964), 81–84; "Pure Theory of Public Expenditure and Taxation" (Mimeographed, September 1966)].

In my own review of Musgrave's treatise, I suggested the relevance of a model that would include goods embodying varying degrees of "publicness," based on a generalization of the external economies notion ["The Theory of Public Finance," *Southern Economic Journal,* XXVI (January 1960), 234–38]. Such a model was developed provisionally by Otto A. Davis and Andrew Whinston ["Some Foundations of Public Expenditure Theory" (Mimeographed, Carnegie Institute of Technology, November 1961)]. J. C. Weldon, in his comment on Breton's paper, expressed the same objective and presented a different model ["Public Goods and Federalism," *Canadian Journal of Economics and Political Science,* XXXII (May 1966), 230–38].

The literature on external economies and diseconomies is, of course, exclusively devoted to analyzing "impure" goods and services. Several relatively recent contributions may be noted here [R. H. Coase, "The Problem of Social Cost," *Journal of Law and Economics,* III (October 1960), 1–44; Otto A. Davis and Andrew Whinston, "Externalities, Welfare, and the Theory of Games," *Journal of Political Economy,* LXX (June 1962), 241–62; James M. Buchanan and Wm. Craig Stubblebine, "Externality," *Economica,* XXIX (November 1962), 371–84; Ralph Turvey, "On Divergencies Between Social Cost and Private Cost," *Economica,* XXX (August 1963), 309–13; E. J. Mishan, "Reflections on Recent Developments in the Concept of External Effects," *Canadian Journal of Economics and Political Science,* XXXI (February 1965), 3–34; Charles Plott, "Externalities and Corrective Taxes," *Economica,* XXXIII (February 1965), 84–87; S. Wellisz, "On External Diseconomies and the Government-Assisted Invisible Hand," *Economica,* XXXI (November 1964), 345–62; Otto A. Davis and Andrew Whinston, "On Externalities, Information, and the Government-Assisted Invisible Hand," *Economica,* XXXIII (August 1966), 303–18; James M. Buchanan and Gordon Tullock, "Public and Private Interaction Under Reciprocal Externality," in *The Public Economy of Urban Communities,* edited by J. Margolis (Resources for the Future, 1965), pp. 52–72].

Specific problems that arise in the determination of the mix of an impure public good have been discussed by Carl Shoup and Douglas Dosser [Shoup, "Standards for Distributing a Free Governmental Service: Crime Prevention," *Public Finance,* XIX (1964), 383–94; Dosser, "Note on Carl S. Shoup's 'Standards for Distributing a Free Governmental Service: Crime Prevention,' " *Public Finance,* ibid., 395–402].

Some aspects of specific consumption externality in education have been analyzed by Mark Pauly ["Mixed Public-Private Financing of Education: Efficiency and Feasibility," *American Economic Review,* LVII (March 1967), 120–30]. In a more general setting, some of these problems have been discussed by Burton Weisbrod [*External Benefits of Public Education* (Princeton: Industrial Relations Section, Princeton University, 1964)].

5. Many Private Goods, Many Persons

The "Free-Rider" Problem

The assumptions of our initial models have been progressively relaxed, and the theory of public goods has become more general in the process. The generalization remains incomplete in essential respects, however, due to the two-person, two-good limitation. Extension to the n-person, n-good cases must now be introduced. Should these final steps prove impossible, some of the earlier simplifications would be of negative rather than positive explanatory value.

From One to N Private Goods

One stage of this remaining generalization is simple. No difficulties arise in shifting our attention from a world where *one* private good and *one* public good exist to a world where there are n private goods and *one* public good. This is the model within which much of the theoretical discussion of public goods demand-supply has taken place. The results are equivalent to those reached in the simplified two-good model. All that is required here is the selection of one from among the n private goods as a *numeraire,* that is, as a money commodity. Once this is done the model reduces to the two-good case as before, with the numeraire becoming a common denominator for all private goods. Actual and potential exchanges can be treated as transfers in the numeraire. In this respect, the "market" for the single public good is not different from that for any single selected nonnumeraire private good. All trades reduce to two-good dimensions. This acknowledged function of the money commodity has been emphasized for its efficiency-promoting results.

The costs of exchange in a money economy are drastically lower than those in any comparable barter system. The dimensional aspect here has not, however, been so fully appreciated for its facilitation of elementary theorizing about the market processes. The use of money allows the economist, who has normally been concerned almost exclusively with private-goods exchange, to possess a "magic number," two, despite all of his sophisticated models covering many commodities.

From One to Many Public Goods

So long as there is one purely private good to serve as a numeraire, no problem arises in generalizing the model to include any number of public goods. Each of the latter can be treated separately and "trade" in this good and the numeraire can be discussed in the same terms as before. Complexities emerge when complementarity and substitutability relationships among public goods are strong, or when institutional arrangements for provision (e.g., general-fund budgeting) force joint considerations. These complexities need not be disturbing for elementary analysis, however, and the standard professional tools of economics can be employed.

The model cannot be generalized to cover the case where *all* goods are public. Here no numeraire private good is available to reduce the analytics to our magic two dimensions, and trade becomes much more complex, both in reality and in analysis. We must resort to something like a generalized barter model. Such a model does have relevance to certain real-world problems, notably those encountered when the theory is applied to certain political-choice situations. This particular extension will be developed separately in Chapter 6. At this point, our analysis will be limited to models that contain at least one numeraire private good.

From Two to Many Persons

The major part of this chapter concerns the dropping of the other half of the restriction on models introduced to this point, that which is imposed on the number of persons or potential trading entities. Here, once again, no problem arises in analyzing trade in private goods, at least no problem that is not thoroughly familiar to the trained economist. As we know, shifting from two-person to *n*-person models facilitates analysis in many respects. In two-person exchange, neither trader confronts alternatives outside the exchange nexus. Each person finds it advantageous to behave strategically, to bargain, since the terms of trade as well as the extent of trade are determined internally to the exchange process. If, however, there exist alternative buyers and sellers, the terms of trade tend to be imposed externally on both parties to any specific exchange. These terms are fixed by all participants indirectly in a large-number market process, and they exogenously set the respective shares in the total gains derived by two traders in any single exchange. Their own decisions, within the narrow confines of this exchange, reduce to agreeing on quantities to be transferred on these given terms. The necessary conditions for full trading equilibrium are identical in *n*-person and in two-person models. But because all traders adjust to common price ratios the *n*-person model is more determinate.

This distinction is illustrated in Figure 5.1, which is again the familiar

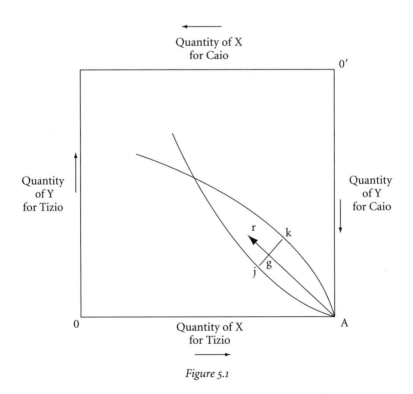

Figure 5.1

Edgeworth-box diagram. Under two-person trade in isolation, the contract locus, *jk,* represents the set of all possible final equilibrium positions, given *A* as the initial point. At each position on this locus, the necessary marginal equalities hold; all gains-from-trade are exhausted. In shifting from *A* toward the contract locus, each trader is motivated to bargain, to behave strategically, in order to secure more favorable distribution of the available spoils. In an *n*-person situation the same two traders would tend to move swiftly along the single ray, *r,* to a unique point, *g,* on the contract locus, the slope of this ray being the price ratio between the two goods. This price is set externally, and, once set, it determines uniquely the solution to the "bargaining game" in which these two players would engage if they were isolated. The price ratio exerts this stabilizing and efficiency-generating influence because it represents the terms upon which each trader may exchange with outsiders, that is with alternative sellers-buyers. Clearly, neither trader will ordinarily give his direct opposite number much better terms than he can secure from others. Most of the structure of neoclassical price theory consists of inferential predictions about characteristics of rays along which exchanges take place; that is, with predictions about prices that will come to be established through the interplay of all the demand-supply elements in *n*-person, *n*-commodity markets.

Perfect Competition

The extension of the model analyzing trade in private goods from two persons to many persons has been oversimplified in the above summary. Full determinateness in the model emerges only when all of the requirements for perfect competition are satisfied. Much of modern analysis assumes at the outset that competition is perfect and then proceeds to derive inferential predictions about the characteristics of equilibrium. Interesting and important questions concerning the path toward final trading equilibrium have been relatively neglected. While there is no doubt but that this methodological procedure has facilitated analysis in many respects, its value in contributing to our understanding of the way market institutions may be predicted to function seems questionable. A more fruitful approach is one in which competitive organization *emerges* as a result of the interaction of demanders and suppliers in markets, instead of being superimposed, as it were, by assumption. This latter approach is necessarily more cumbersome and complex, and all ideas about uniqueness of solution must be jettisoned. There exist many paths toward final equilibrium; there is some scope for bargaining behavior in almost every trading situation. Prices come to be established in a process of moving toward an ever-changing equilibrium; they are not "solved for," computer-style, exogenous of behavior in markets and then subsequently "announced."

This approach concentrates on exchange as such. And even in a world where many persons mutually trade among themselves in many private goods, all exchange is still two-sided. The economist can still call up his magic number, two. In each exchange, there is one selling unit and one buying unit; each trade is bilateral. In this sense, usage of the term "multilateral" by economists is often misleading. The emergence of a money commodity, a numeraire, allows the whole trading process, however many persons and many goods it may involve, to be factored down, so to speak, into an intersecting set of two-person, two-good exchanges.

The limitation on strategic behavior, on bargaining, is imposed by the availability of alternatives, actual and potential. To the extent that effective alternatives exist, the prospects of productive returns from investment in strategy are reduced. In the extreme, expected returns do not equal costs even at the zero margin. Each of us faces this situation in standard American retail markets. We confront single sellers, but we do not normally find it worthwhile to bargain over prices. The seller, because he has alternative buyers, will not readily respond to below-list offers. However, because buyers also have access to alternative sellers, the single seller cannot readily put his own prices above those charged by others. Alternatives impose external limits on the two-person, two-good trade in private goods, and the effectiveness of these alternatives measures the efficiency of the market structure.

The purpose of all this is not to present a discourse on the theory of markets. The point emphasized is that so long as we restrict analysis to trade in private goods, we do not effectively change dimensions in shifting from the grossly simplified two-person, two-commodity model to one that contains many persons and many goods. Such a shift adds determinateness to the results because the terms of trade are affected by potential as well as actual exchange. Since each trader can independently adjust his quantities of private goods, as demander or supplier, there is no necessity of introducing n-party exchange models explicitly.

N Persons and "Trade" in a Single Public Good

This characteristic of independent quantity adjustment greatly facilitates both trade and theorizing about trade. When a public good is introduced, parties can no longer adjust quantities independently. As the analysis of earlier chapters has shown, we can define the characteristics of trading equilibrium, even here, so long as we stay in the two-person model. As we add more parties to such a model, however, and as we shift from the two-person toward an n-person case, we do not secure the same efficiency as in the world where trade is limited exclusively to private goods. With public-goods exchange, *all* relevant parties must be brought directly into the contract. The economist's magic number fails, and no amount of sophisticated theorizing can really factor down the trading process into a set of intersecting two-party exchanges. Genuine n-person trade must be analyzed for the first time, and the "solution" must reflect agreement among all of the n trading partners.

The problem may be discussed in terms of agreement. Return to trade in purely private goods. This trade requires explicit agreement between only two persons in each exchange, a buyer and a seller, along with the implicit agreement or acquiescence on the part of the other $n-2$ members of the group. Private goods trade involves *implicit unanimity,* in the sense that parties external to each particular exchange allow the two traders involved to remain undisturbed in their dealings. Institutional arrangements are, of course, designed to prevent such interference by external parties, but these institutions themselves emerge from a recognition of the underlying realities of most exchanges. Unless such implicit unanimity is present, external parties can prevent any proposed exchange by offering more attractive terms to one of the two traders. It is this particular characteristic of competitive economic order that allows it to satisfy the familiar necessary marginal conditions for Pareto optimality. Trade in private goods will proceed so long as mutual gains remain unexploited, and so long as this requirement of implicit unanimity is met. Implicit unanimity is not imposed, however, on private-goods trade; it is a characteristic of such trade.

In our previous analysis of Tizio-Caio trades, the motivation for agreement on supplying the public good was shown to be equivalent to that for engaging in ordinary private-goods trade. Mutual gains can be secured through mutual agreement. The same motivation holds when we add more persons to the model; unexploited gains-from-trade will be present so long as persons who place any positive marginal evaluation on the public good remain outside the range of agreement. To show this in a three-person case, let us add Sempronio to the Tizio-Caio illustration. Suppose that Sempronio desires to migrate to the island, and that he, like the others, will share equally in the benefits of any mosquito repelling activity. Tizio and Caio will not be willing to allow Sempronio to join them unless he contributes some share in the costs of this public good, either through direct production on his own account or indirectly through transfers to them of private goods. Sempronio will, presumably, be prepared to make some contribution toward this end. He cannot, however, simply engage in ordinary exchange with either Tizio or Caio. The two-party agreement between Tizio and Caio on the quantity of public good to be jointly supplied must now become a genuine three-party agreement in a direct and explicit sense. Each person will now have to consider his own contribution in relation to each of the other two persons and to both combined. The extension to four, five and on to *n* persons similarly will require further inclusion in the range of *explicit* agreement. Such agreement is necessary in all instances where decisions are made on the amount of public good to be supplied jointly for all relevant members of the group.

The most obvious inference to be drawn from this preliminary discussion concerns the predicted increase in the costs of reaching agreement as the number of parties in contract expands. Two-party bargains may be difficult enough, especially when the gains-from-trade are large. Three-party bargains are probably proportionately more difficult still to arrange. As the size of the inclusive group becomes large, explicit agreement among all members may actually become almost prohibitively costly. It is essential to understand precisely why this is true. Herein lies the explanation of the failure of market-like or exchange organization to function effectively in supplying public goods that jointly supply large groups. Also here is provided the explanation for the emergence of indirect trade via the mechanism of collective-coercive arrangements.

Strictly Strategic Behavior—The Small-Number Case

When *all* members of a group must reach agreement, and there is no external contact with others outside the group, there are no external limitations on the terms of trade among these members. This holds for two-person, few-person and many-person groups. It is necessary, however, to distinguish carefully the behavior of the individual participant in a small-number setting and that of the same individual in a large-number setting. Rational behavior will be quite different in these two cases, despite the presence of the same general sort of mutual interdependence. In small-group situations, each potential trader is motivated to behave strategically, to bargain, in an attempt to secure for himself differentially favorable terms. At the same time, he will also seek to promote general agreement so as to secure the advantages of the acknowledged mutual gains. Here the trader expects through his own action to modify the behavior of fellow traders in the group. He will try to predict as best he can the response of these others to his own action, and he will then select that combination of action and predicted response that maximizes his expected utility. He is in an acknowledged gaming situation. He may deliberately resort to strategic "antisocial" behavior even though he recognizes that mutual gains can be secured from cooperative behavior. It is in this small-number model that strictly strategic behavior on the part of the participant becomes fully rational. Here the individual will find it to his advantage to conceal his true preferences and to give false signals about those preferences to his opponents-partners.

This small-number case has been exhaustively analyzed by game theorists, although wholly satisfying results have not extended beyond the level of two-person, constant-sum games. The several approaches need not be elaborated here since these models are *not* those most appropriate for analyzing *n*-person "trades" in public goods. Normally, political groups are organized so as to include many persons. Our analysis must, therefore, be confined primarily to the large-number case.

General Interdependence—The Large-Number Case

The individual, as a member of a large group characterized by general interdependence among all of its members, will not expect to influence the behavior of other individuals through his own actions. He will not behave strategically; he will not bargain; he will not "game." Instead, he will simply adjust his own behavior to the behavior of "others," taken as a composite unit without the anticipation that their behavior may change. He accepts the totality of others' action as a parameter for his own decisions, as a part of his environment, a part of nature, so to speak, and he does not consider this subject to variation as a result of his own behavior, directly or indirectly.

A familiar reference to orthodox price theory will make the distinction between the small-number and the large-number case clear. In a duopoly or oligopoly situation, the rational firm tries to predict the response of its rivals to its own actions. In a competitive setting, by contrast, the firm accepts the behavior of its "rivals," as a datum, and simply reacts to its environment. The underlying interdependence through the market is the same in both instances, but the difference in numbers generates basic differences in the behavior patterns of rational decision makers. In the large-number model, the individual considers the influence of his own action, relative to the totality of action generated by the group within which he operates to be so small as not to affect at all the aggregative results. Hence, he reasons, and correctly, that he had best ignore altogether the reactions of others (separately or as a subgroup) to his own possible "antisocial" behavior.

The psychology of behavior differs in the two situations. In small-group interaction, the individual recognizes interdependence in a specifically personalized sense. He will be directly conscious of rivalry; he will (in situations where the numbers exceed two) be motivated to form coalitions. He will recognize the productivity of joint action with one or more of his fellows. *Vis-à-vis* each other person in the group, the individual will sense a relationship of both competition and cooperation. All of this disappears in the large-number situation. The individual may fully acknowledge the mutual interdependence among all members at some logical, analytical level of discourse. But he will not find it productive to seek out and form coalitions with his fellows to the extent evidenced in the small-number case. He will not consider himself either competing or cooperating with other members of the group. There is no personalized relationship of interdependence here, no scope for bargaining to obtain favorable terms of trade since, for each person, these terms are exogenously fixed. This removal of bargaining opportunities has its obverse, however, in that no trades will be arranged either.

The small-number case provides the individual with motivation both to initiate trade and to bargain over terms. The effective large-number case, where interdependence is general and cannot be factored down, tends to eliminate both trading and bargaining behavior.

In the large-number setting, individuals find it rational to act independently, despite the fact that the composite result of individual and independent action is nonoptimal for each and every person in the group, and this may well be recognized as such.

Public-Goods Supply and "Free Riders"

When the large-number dilemma summarized above exists, the natural processes of trade, the emergence of market-like institutions, cannot be predicted to generate shifts toward optimality. Gains from n-person trade or agreement are clearly present, and these potentialities may be universally recognized. But market-like arrangements cannot readily materialize due to the absence of notable gains from two-person or small-number exchanges.

In such situations, individuals will suggest n-person "rules" or "arrangements" aimed explicitly at reducing or eliminating the inefficiencies generated by independent behavior. In a very broad sense, agreements on such rules can also be classified as "trades." It may prove almost impossible, however, to secure agreement among a large number of persons, and to enforce such agreements as are made. The reason for this lies in the "free-rider" position in which each individual finds himself. While he may recognize that similar independent behavior on the part of everyone produces undesirable results, it is not to his own interest to enter voluntarily into an agreement since, for him, optimal results can be attained by allowing others to supply the public good to the maximum extent while he enjoys a "free ride"; that is, secures the benefits without contributing toward the costs. Even if an individual should enter into such a cost-sharing agreement, he will have a strong incentive to break his own contract, to chisel on the agreed terms.

It is worth noting that there are no personal elements in the individual's calculus of decision here, and, for this reason, the "free-rider" terminology so often used in public-goods theory is itself somewhat misleading. The individual is caught in a dilemma by the nature of his situation; he has no sensation of securing benefits at the expense of others in any personal manner.

And to the extent that all persons act similarly, no one does secure such benefits. Free rider, literally interpreted, more closely describes the small-number model, in which the individual does compete explicitly with others in a personal sense. Here, "let George do it" means just that, with George fully identified. But the small-number model is not appropriate for analyzing the theory of public goods. In the relevant large-number setting, the individual does not really say to himself, "let George do it"; he simply treats others as a part of nature. The "prisoners' dilemma," which has been analyzed at length in game theory, is more descriptive of the large-number behavioral setting, but, even here, this dilemma has normally been developed in two-person models. In such models, nonoptimality arises because of the mutual distrust and noncommunication between the prisoners, which are once again personal relationships. In the large-number or n-person dilemma, the failure to attain desirable results through independent action is analytically equivalent to the orthodox prisoners' dilemma, but without the personal overtones. Full communication among all persons in a large-number dilemma will still not remove the inefficiency in results.

The organization and enforcement of efficient institutional arrangements will rarely be possible unless *all* persons are somehow brought into potential agreement. The alternative of remaining outside the agreement, or remaining a free rider, must be effectively eliminated before the individual can appropriately weigh the comparative advantages of independent behavior on the one hand and cooperative action on the other. It is because they facilitate the elimination of this free-rider alternative that coercive arrangements, governmental in nature, tend to emerge from the preferences of individuals themselves, at least on some conceptual level of constitution-making. Once the possibility or opportunity of behaving as a free rider is removed from an individual's range of effective choice, he can then select among the remaining alternatives on more meaningful terms of comparative efficiency, at least in an ideal sense. His behavior under these more restricted conditions will be discussed more fully later in the chapter. Before this, however, it will be useful to show why, in the large-number case, the individual will not contribute voluntarily to the costs of public goods, at least not in an amount sufficiently large to generate optimal levels of provision. The analysis in the following section is redundant in one sense, but, as suggested earlier, varied iteration can serve pedagogic purpose.

A Probabilistic Approach to the Free Rider's Choice

Consider first a community of 1000 persons in which it is widely known that a fixed-facility purely public good, if constructed, will yield benefits valued at $10 per person, or $10,000 in total. It is also widely known that the facility can be constructed for $5000.

Each individual examines his choice alternatives, which he considers as: (1) contribute a share in the joint cost of the undertaking, or (2) contribute nothing. How will he rank these alternatives? If he predicts that others in the group will contribute an amount sufficient to finance the facility, he can obviously gain from not contributing. If he predicts that others in the group will not contribute, he gains nothing by contributing himself because of the indivisibility of the benefits. In view of the large-number setting, the individual does not predict that his own behavior can influence others in the group. There will be no difference in his predictions as to the aggregate behavior of others whether or not he contributes a share of his own. In this sort of situation, regardless of how the individual estimates the behavior of others, he must always rationally choose the free-rider alternative. Since all individuals will tend to act similarly, the facility will not be constructed from proceeds of wholly voluntary contributions of potential beneficiaries.

This situation may be illustrated in the simple matrix shown as Figure 5.2. Values to the individual under the different combinations are taken from the numerical example. The terms in brackets represent probabilities assigned to each of the possible behavior patterns of others. The important thing to note is that these probabilities do not change from one row to the other. This being the case, any set of probability coefficients will give the same result. The highest expected value will always be assigned to the row labeled "Not Contribute."

	"Others" Contribute	"Others" Do Not Contribute	Expected Value
Individual Contributes	$ 5 (.5)	− $5 (.5)	0
Individual Does Not Contribute	$10 (.5)	0 (.5)	$5

Figure 5.2

This situation, relevant to the large-number setting, may be sharply contrasted with that present in a small-number case. Under the same general conditions as before, assume now that the community contains 10 persons. Each person now anticipates a total benefit of $1000 and a *pro rata* cost share of $500. He will face the same alternatives as before; he can contribute or he can refrain from contributing. However, in this small-number setting, where personal interaction is recognized, the individual may consider that his own action will exert some influence on the behavior of others in the group. If he contributes nothing, he may assess the probability of noncooperation on the part of others higher than if he contributes some share. This change alone may be sufficient, on rational grounds, to cause him to contribute. In terms of the small-number example introduced above, the situation is summarized in Figure 5.3. Note that the probability assignments do vary from row to row; the individual predicts that his own behavior will influence that of others. This is why, as shown in this example, the expected value is higher when the individual contributes than when he does not. Whether or not this result will be forthcoming depends, of course, on the specific assignment of probabilities. The individual may consider that his own action in contribution will lower, not increase, the probability of others' making contributions of their own. In this case, the shift in probabilities between rows would be the reverse of that indicated in Figure 5.3. This situation is illustrated in Figure 5.4, which indicates that the individual attains a higher expected value by not making than by making voluntary contribution to the cost of the public-goods facility. Here the individual is quite specifically acting like a free rider. He anticipates that others will offset or compensate for his own antisocial behavior. Whether or not conditions are like those shown in Figure 5.3 or Figure 5.4 will depend, in part, on the power of sanction that the group exerts over the individual. Since the whole analysis applies only for *small* groups, the inter-

	"Others" Contribute	"Others" Do Not Contribute	Expected Value
Individual Contributes	$ 500 (.8)	− $500 (.2)	$300
Individual Does Not Contribute	$1000 (.2)	0 (.8)	$200

Figure 5.3

	"Others" Contribute	*"Others" Do Not* Contribute	*Expected* Value
Individual Contributes	$ 500 (.8)	− $500 (.2)	$300
Individual Does Not Contribute	$1000 (.9)	0 (.1)	$900

Figure 5.4

action is likely to be personal, and the possibility of excluding genuine non-conformists will normally be present. This suggests that the situation depicted in Figure 5.3 is more likely to occur than that depicted in Figure 5.4.

In both the large-number and the small-number examples, we have assumed a certain lumpiness or indivisibility in the public-goods facility. This insures that no production will be forthcoming under wholly voluntary behavior in the large-number case, and perhaps none in the small-number case. In order to make the analysis fully comparable to the models introduced earlier, this assumption of lumpiness must be dropped. If we now assume that the public good can be produced in fully divisible units, some quantity may be forthcoming even in the large-number setting. An independent-adjustment equilibrium will be established with some positive production even if this remains small relative to the Pareto-optimal output under normal circumstances.

The probabilistic approach makes the distinction between individual behavior in the large-number and the small-number setting clear. There is, of course, no *a priori* means of determining just what size a group must be in order to bring about the basic shift in any individual's behavior pattern. This will vary from one individual to another, even for members of the same group. The critical limit is imposed by the personal relationship that the individual feels with his fellows in negotiation. During periods of extreme stress, such as was apparently evidenced by the British during World War II, behavior characteristic of small groups may have extended over almost the whole population. In other situations, when such cohesive forces do not exist, and when commonly shared goals are not apparent, individuals may behave as they would in large groups, even for quite limited community actions. Variations in custom, tradition, in ethical standards; all these serve to shift the critical limits between small-group and large-group behavior. This has, of course, been recognized by economists. The number of firms necessary to insure genuine competition is acknowledged to vary widely with many relevant determining variables.

Wicksell's Unanimity Rule

When there exists general public-goods interdependence among many persons, the independent behavior of separate individuals will not generate shifts toward Pareto-efficient outcomes. The rules for behavior must somehow be modified. Knut Wicksell was the first scholar to recognize this, and he proposed specific changes in the setting within which individual choices are made. The free-rider motivation is eliminated only when the individual is made aware that this own choice among alternatives *does* affect, and in some positive and measurable sense, the outcomes for *others* in the group, even if the membership is large. To accomplish this, Wicksell proposed that group decisions on public-goods supply be made *unanimously*.

Note precisely what the requirement of unanimity does. Knowing that *all* persons in the group must agree before a decision becomes effective, the individual now chooses an outcome, not only for himself, but also for each and all of his fellows. He is confronted with the stark fact that remaining a free rider is impossible. He cannot behave independent of the group. If he refuses to agree to a specific proposal, he cannot expect others to proceed with its implementation. His refusal to accept a proffered scheme for the whole group means that this particular scheme will not come into being; he cannot expect the benefits without their corresponding costs.

In its practical effect on the individual's behavior, the unanimity rule converts the large-number case into a small-number case. Under this requirement, the effective size of the group is reduced to two parties; the individual considers himself to be trading with "all others" as a unit. The free rider is wholly eliminated, but the difficulties that arise in the small-number case are reintroduced to an extent. There is scope for bargaining, for strategic behavior, for gaming, in the explicit sense, behavior that is wholly missing from the *n*-person situation under independent action. Despite these problems, strong motivation exists for the individual to engage in trade, and some approach to the Paretian efficiency frontier may be predicted to take place.

Let us examine somewhat more carefully the situation of the individual under an effective rule of unanimity. A proposal is made, let us say, to supply X units of a public good at a total tax charge of Y dollars on each person. Assume for the moment that the benefits of this proposed quantity exceed the costs for the reference person whose calculus we are considering. He will secure some net taxpayer's surplus if the proposal is adopted by the group. He may, however, vote against the proposal under certain conditions. He will do so if he anticipates that, after defeat of the proposal (which his own vote can insure), a different proposal will be presented that will yield him higher net benefits and which stands some chance of being adopted. Each person is, in a sense, involved in an ordinary two-party bargaining game with all others, whom he considers as a unit.

Important elements of the large-number case remain in this situation, however, elements that reduce substantially the motivation for strictly strategic behavior. Shifts toward the Pareto frontier are, therefore, more predictable here than in genuine two-party bargaining situations. To an extent, the individual must consider any proposal to be exogenously presented. He will not attribute the proposal to a specific bargaining party, as a person, since the party he confronts exists only in the "all others" form. The individual will not predict that his own strategy will exert much, if any, influence on the behavior of his "trading partner." He remains, in this sense, in the large-number case. By refusing to accept the terms implicit in a proposal, he will not consider himself to be influencing substantially the terms of subsequent proposals that will be put forward. He will not think that he is necessarily empowered, through his refusal to accept a proposal, to suggest alternative ones that provide him with more favorable terms. He may think of proposals as being advanced almost at random with the order quite independent of his own actions. There will always remain the probability that a proposal subsequently introduced would be more favorable than the one under consideration, but this probability will not be significantly changed by his own refusal to accept any particular proposal that is presented.

In view of these characteristics of the situation, the individual will tend to vote favorably on proposals that provide him with net benefits, and which also allocate total costs among all persons in a manner that he considers to be "fair," "just" or "equitable." These essentially ethical considerations become important for the individual's own calculus of choice here because they influence his own predictions as to the success or failure of subsequent proposals. Assume, for example, that a collective group is composed of individuals roughly equivalent in economic position. A proposal is advanced to finance, from the proceeds of a head tax, a public good known to provide general benefits. Assume further that each person will secure some net benefits. In this situation, an individual is likely to vote for the proposal. If he places all others in his own position, he will recognize that symmetry or fairness in the distribution of costs is a relevant factor in his choice.

Note that the behavior here is not the same as that discussed under the generalization principle in ethics. This latter principle states that an individual should act favorably on a proposal if he considers the results to be favorable should all others act similarly. What the unanimity requirement does is to force all others to act, if not similarly, at least as laid down in the specifics of the proposal presented. The distribution of costs among all persons is specified in the proposition. The generalization principle in ethics, as a norm for voluntary behavior, fails in large-number groups for precisely free-rider reasons. Wicksell's emendation takes the form of a general rule, to be imposed on everyone, that the individual may rationally support.

While the elements of the large-number case that remain under an effective unanimity rule tend to make the average or representative individual choose among alternatives in some nonstrategic sense, such behavior cannot be generalized to *all* members of a large group. However, the nature of the unanimity rule is such that group decisions are impossible unless *all* persons agree. A single negative vote blocks a proposal, even if all others in the group approve it. To the extent that participants fully appreciate their own individual blocking power, some negative votes could be predicted with almost any conceivable proposal that might be put forward, regardless of the net benefits provided to each person and regardless of symmetry or fairness properties. Practically speaking, the rule of unanimity would result in few, if any, decisions being made.

Again Wicksell recognized this, and he modified his scheme to allow for some departure from complete unanimity, for which he substituted "relative unanimity," relatively unanimous approval, by which he seems to have meant some five-sixths of the total membership. Note precisely what this qualification of the rule accomplishes. So long as the individual knows, in advance, that his own vote, standing alone, cannot effectively block a proposal, he will not be motivated to exploit others for his own uniquely differential benefit.

If a proposal is presented for a vote that embodies net benefits for him, he will tend to accept it, even if under a rule of full unanimity, he would be tempted to block the same issue. Under relative unanimity, it seems probable that a sufficient number of individuals would behave nonstrategically to allow collective decisions on public goods to be reached. Interestingly, under relative unanimity we might predict that proposals embodying symmetry in solution would, on occasion, be adopted unanimously, whereas the same proposals, under full unanimity as the voting rule, would be rejected. This suggests that Wicksell's purpose in partially relaxing the unanimity rule was not that of allowing for the overruling of a recalcitrant or "nonsocial" minority. Instead the purpose was that of modifying the conditions for choice for each member of the group in a way that eliminates from serious consideration the possibility of securing uniquely discriminatory benefits.

The Unanimity Rule and Pareto Optimality

The opportunities for bargaining, for strategic behavior, under the rule of unanimity, or relative unanimity, arise only for inframarginal proposals supplying-financing public goods. To relate our discussion of individual choice behavior in large groups operating under a unanimity rule to that of the earlier two-person trading model, we must assume that the public good or service can be provided in continuously variable quantities and that proposals will be made which allow for such continuous variation. On inframarginal units, net taxpayers' surplus arises, and this provides the scope for bargaining behavior. The final distribution of the gains among separate persons will depend, in part, on the order of presentation of proposals. There is nothing in the institution of unanimity to determine the distribution of these gains analogous to the working of markets. As the margin is approached, the net surplus tends to be squeezed out, and at the margin itself no gains-from-trade remain. The number of proposals that can secure relatively unanimous approval is continually reduced as the margin is approached, and, at the last stage, only *one* proposal for distributing the costs of an incremental addition to the quantity of a public good (given the manner of distribution of net gains over inframarginal units) can secure genuine unanimity. When the Pareto conditions are satisfied, by definition, no proposal for change can secure the consent of all parties. The converse also applies. From any position that does not satisfy the Pareto conditions, there must exist changes that can secure the approval of all persons in the group, bargaining difficulties aside.

The necessary relaxation of the unanimity rule in the strict sense and its replacement by the rule of relative unanimity or qualified majority involves some cost in efficiency. Strictly speaking, there is no assurance that the Pareto frontier will be attained under any rule short of full unanimity if side payments in money are not allowed. Proposals which must secure the support of only five-sixths of the total number of persons in a group may be adopted and still be nonoptimal, and departures from Pareto positions may take place under such a rule.

Only a partial escape from this dilemma seems possible. If the rule for making decisions is separated from the observer's evaluation of collective decision-making, it becomes possible to rank all such decisions in terms of their efficiency. As shown above, some departure from strict unanimity is necessary to reduce the scope for strategic bargaining behavior by the individual and to insure that group decisions do, in fact, get made. Once the rule for decision-making is chosen, however, the relative efficiency of different collective outcomes can be measured in terms of the percentage of total membership that agrees. If, under some relative unanimity or qualified majority rule (or even under simple-majority rule) a proposal receives unanimous support of all parties, the observer can label the move as "efficient" in the full Pareto sense. In this way, given any decision rule, he can array various voting outcomes in terms of the percentage of votes cast in their favor. The proportion of positive votes becomes an acceptable criterion for the efficiency of separate proposals.

The Unanimity Rule and Real-World Institutions

Knut Wicksell produced an escape from the free-rider dilemma inherent in the large-number, public-goods interdependence. If the rule of unanimity should be applied, even in a relative or qualified sense, public goods will tend to be supplied efficiently. Analytically, this Wicksellian contribution provides a major step toward the development of a theory of the demand and the supply of public goods and services. In terms of the institutions through which choices are made in the real world, however, more relevant theory is yet required. To some extent, the Wicksellian contribution serves much the same function here as the economist's assumption of perfect competition in the theory of private-goods demand and supply. There is a major difference between the two devices, however, and this must be recognized. Again to an extent, something approaching the descriptive meaning of perfect competition can be shown to emerge from the interaction of individuals engaged in private market processes. Rarely will Wicksellian choice-making institutions emerge naturally from the rational decisions of individuals, even when we consider the appropriate stages of constitutional choice. Real-world observations suggest that considerations other than simple efficiency must loom large in dictating the rules for collective decision-making. The Wicksellian device is helpful, however, in establishing a benchmark from which possible sacrifices of first-order economic efficiency can be measured, at least conceptually. Subsequent chapters will explore some of the issues involved in developing a theory of public goods that seems better for explaining real-world events.

Bibliographical Appendix

In his fundamental contribution to the theory of public finance, Knut Wicksell noted the predicted failure of voluntary individual behavior to generate efficient outcomes in the presence of public-goods phenomena. [*Finanztheoretische Untersuchungen* (Jena: Gustav Fischer, 1896). A major portion of this essay is translated as: "A New Principle of Just Taxation," and included in *Classics in the Theory of Public Finance,* edited by R. A. Musgrave and A. T. Peacock (London: Macmillan, 1958), pp. 72–118.] In his later model, Erik Lindahl was perhaps less perceptive than Wicksell concerning the difficulties in any voluntaristic solution. [*Die Gerechtigkeit des Besteuerung* (Lund, 1919). A major portion of this essay is translated as: "Just Taxation—A Positive Solution," and included in *Classics in the Theory of Public Finance,* pp. 168–76.] Later essays by Lindahl should also be noted ["Some Controversial Questions in the Theory of Taxation," originally written in German and published in 1928, and published in translation and included in, *Classics in the Theory of Public Finance,* pp. 214–32; also, "Tax Principles and Tax Policy," *International Economic Papers,* No. 10 (London: Macmillan, 1959), pp. 7–23].

In his early critical review of Lindahl's model, R. A. Musgrave stressed the failure of the voluntary-exchange mechanism ["The Voluntary Exchange Theory of Public Economy," *Quarterly Journal of Economics,* LIII (February 1939), 213–37]. In his later, and somewhat more favorable, treatment of the Lindahl model, Musgrave emphasized the difficulties in getting individuals to reveal their true preferences in voluntary exchanges involving genuinely public goods [*The Theory of Public Finance* (New York: McGraw-Hill, 1959), Ch. 4]. This aspect of the problem was also stressed by Paul A. Samuelson in his initial paper ["The Pure Theory of Public Expenditure," *Review of Economics and Statistics,* XXXVI (November 1954), 387–89]. Some of the ambiguities involved in the whole "free-rider" notion are sensed by Ansel M. Sharp and Donald R. Escarraz although they do not fully succeed in removing them ["A Reconsideration of the Price or Exchange Theory of Public Finance," *Southern Economic Journal,* XXXI (October 1964), 132–39].

The analysis of the free-rider problem was clarified by Otto A. Davis and Andrew Whinston, especially as concerns the failure of individuals to reveal their preferences ["Some Foundations of Public Expenditure Theory" (Mimeographed, Carnegie Institute of Technology, November 1961)]. Mancur Olson discussed the free-rider problem in some detail and extended the analysis to the problem of the viability of organizations [*The Logic of Collective Action* (Cambridge: Harvard University Press, 1965)]. Olson and Richard Zeckhauser have also applied essentially the same analysis to international sharing problems ["An Economic Theory of Alliances," *Review of Economics and Statistics,* XLVII (August 1966), 266–79]. J. F. Besson has applied the analysis to issues of centralized versus decentralized planning, and he has also provided a good general summary of existing public-goods theory ["Centralisation et decentralisation: Le problème des biens collectifs," *Revue Economique* (No. 4, 1966), 560–602]. Albert Breton has also attempted to relate the theory of public goods to the theory of collective decision-making ["A Theory of Demand for Public Goods," *Canadian Journal of Economics and Political Science,* XXXII (November 1966), 455–67].

The problems of deriving norms for behavior in a voluntaristic ethics are closely related to those discussed in this chapter. M. A. Singer provided a modern discussion of the generalization principle [*Generalization in Ethics* (New York: Alfred A. Knopf, 1961)]. The necessity of distinguishing between the generalization argument and the argument in favor of establishing general rules was pointed out by Neil A. Dorman ["The Refutation of the Generalization Argument," *Ethics,* LXXIV (January 1964), 150–54]. Some of the specific relationships between the ethical discussion and the economic one were treated, along with the necessity of distinguishing behavior in the small-number and the large-number cases, in my own paper ["Ethical Rules, Expected Values, and Large Numbers," *Ethics*, LXXVI (October 1965), 1–13].

The free-rider problem in public-goods theory is an example of what may properly be called a "large-number prisoners' dilemma," a problem that is pervasive in many areas of economic theory. For a good general discussion of the prisoners' dilemma in the two-person model, the treatment by R. Duncan Luce and Howard Raiffa is recommended [*Games and Decisions* (New York: John Wiley and Sons, 1957), pp. 94–101]. Much of the analysis concerned with the competitiveness of alternative industrial structures is devoted, directly or indirectly, to the same issue. The "theory of chiseling" on cartel agreements is essentially the "theory of the free rider" in reverse. [For an interesting discussion on the former, see G. Warren Nutter, "Duopoly, Oligopoly, and Emerging Competition," *Southern Economic Journal*, XXX (April 1964), 342–52).]

In two separate works, independently and jointly written, I have examined some of the implications of Wicksell's proposals for institutional reform, notably his proposal for the rule of unanimity or near-unanimity ["Positive Economics, Welfare Economics, and Political Economy," included in *Fiscal Theory and Political Economy* (Chapel Hill: University of North Carolina Press, 1960), pp. 105–24, and the book written jointly with Gordon Tullock, *The Calculus of Consent* (Ann Arbor: University of Michigan Press, 1962)].

6. Many Public Goods, Many Persons
The World Without a Numeraire

The analysis has been progressively generalized, and we have advanced some distance beyond the simple exchange models initially presented. From two persons in a trading situation to many persons in a political structure: This progression has been partially completed. From one private good to many goods, public and private: This, too, has been accomplished. There remains only the extension to the world where many public goods exist.

The inclusion of many public goods creates no difficulty so long as *one* wholly divisible private good exists that can serve as a unit of account. In this case, each public good (or bundle of goods) can be analyzed separately. Nothing need be added to the formal theoretical structure developed for the single good, although relationships of complementarity and substitutability among public goods themselves would have to be taken into account.

This chapter introduces the quite different problem that arises when no fully divisible private good exists, when there is no numeraire that can be used in trades among separate persons. The purpose is to analyze behavior when *all* goods are "public" in the sense that all members of the interacting group must adjust to the same quantity of each good. This is the world of pure publicness, the world of universal externality, the world of reverse laissez-faire, where nothing can be done independently by an individual.

This model will seem bizarre and wholly unreal especially to economists. The world of pure publicness is rarely encountered even in the most abstruse of mathematical models, because of the rescuing feature contained in the single private-good numeraire. The analysis will, nonetheless, be of value beyond that of pure intellectual exercise. Important real-world decisions on resource allocation may be made without resort to a private-good or money numeraire, and, to the extent that these decisions exist, the analysis is highly relevant. These decisions are likely to be made politically, not through markets or quasi-markets. The models introduced in this chapter will, therefore, be helpful in bridging the gap between the theoretical analysis of economics and the theoretical analysis of politics. A major element in any treatment of "the demand and supply of public goods" is missing until and unless "public" decision-making is included.

Two Persons, One Public Good

Let us first examine a two-person model where there is only one good and this good is purely public. By "purely public" I mean only that each of the two persons in the group must adjust to the *same* quantity. As earlier analysis has shown, by proper definition, any good, descriptively characterized, can be treated as purely public in the sense used here. The model and those that follow can be more fully appreciated if simple illustration is provided, so long as the purpose is recognized to be that of illustration only.

As before, consider two persons, Tizio and Caio, but let us now say that they are university students who find themselves assigned to share the same dormitory room. Their situation requires an agreement or decision on *one* variable, the setting of the thermostat that determines the room temperature. Both men must adjust to the same setting; it is physically impossible for Tizio to enjoy the warmth of a 75° reading, while, at the same time, Caio enjoys the cool comfort of a 65° reading.

If the two men should have identical ordinal utility functions, no decision problem would arise. They would agree immediately and without conflict on a single unique value for the temperature setting. If, however, they should have different utility functions, they will disagree, and some way must be found to make a decision. The problem is illustrated in Figure 6.1. The "quantity of public good," in this case, room temperature settings, is measured along the horizontal axis, and the ordinal preference rankings of the two persons along the vertical axis. Curve P_t shows Tizio's preference rankings, while curve P_c shows the same for Caio. Note that Tizio's most desired setting is at T_t, while Caio's most desired setting is at T_c.

The range of conflict or disagreement is shown between T_t and T_c as ex-

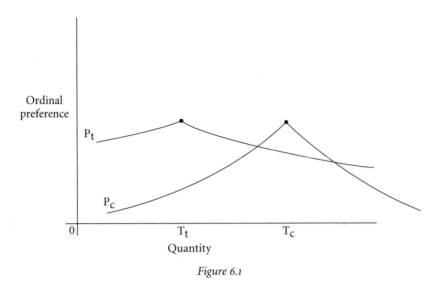

Figure 6.1

tremes. If the initial setting should be either below or above these two limits, the two persons would agree quickly to move to some point within this range. Once settled at a point along this range, however, the situation becomes one of pure conflict. Since by our assumption, there is no numeraire, no side payments or trades can be arranged, and the location of a final solution within this range will be arbitrary. It will depend largely on the skill and strength of the parties to the decision. There is no direct way, in this model, for the relative intensities of preference of the two parties to be expressed. Tizio may be relatively indifferent about room temperature over a considerable range, whereas Caio may be highly sensitive to differences in temperature. If side payments in a numeraire could, in fact, be made, this difference in relative intensities could be expressed and Caio's more intense desires manifested. Without such a numeraire, no such result is predictable.

The two men may, of course, agree on some rule for making the final decision, such as flipping a coin each day to determine who shall decide, or, more likely perhaps, splitting the difference between their two preferred settings.

Many Persons, One Public Good

Few difficulties are encountered in extending this model to include more than two persons. As more persons are added, the range of extreme values for preferred or desired positions is likely to be extended. Again there will be no means of individual expression for relative intensity of preference, and the final rule for decision must be arbitrary, in some sense.

This model, which may seem highly unreal in the two-person context, has considerable real-world relevance in the many-person version. It is precisely this model which many political scientists more or less implicitly assume in their discussion of voting processes. If individuals in referenda, or their representatives in legislative assemblies, are expected to reach agreement on *only one issue* and to do so in complete isolation from all other issues, this is the basic model for analysis.

If specific rules for making decisions are postulated, determinate results can be predicted. For example, if simple-majority voting prevails, the outcome will be that most desired or preferred by the voter whose preference curve reaches its peak at the median among all such peaks arrayed as in Figure 6.1 (see Figure 6.4 below). The stability of this outcome is guaranteed if all preference curves are single-peaked, like those in Figure 6.1. If curves cannot be arrayed in single-peaked fashion, the outcome of majority voting is not normally stable, and the familiar cyclical majority problem arises. This problem will be more fully analyzed later in this chapter.

Two Persons, Two Public Goods

Consider the Tizio-Caio model again, but this time with two public goods rather than one. What differences in result will the introduction of a second public good make? In addition to the thermostat setting, a decision must be made on the time to turn the lights out each evening; and, again, both persons must adjust to the same value also for this variable.

For simplicity in the initial geometrical exposition, let us assume that the two "public goods" are completely independent, one from the other, in both utility functions. There are no relationships of complementarity or substitutability. Neither Tizio nor Caio will desire to modify his optimally preferred temperature with a change as to the time for lights-out.

If the two-person group tries to arrive at a decision on the second common variable, lights-out time, separately from the decision on temperature, we can think of a range of conflict, such as that already shown for temperature in Figure 6.1, if the two utility functions differ with respect to this second variable. The whole situation can be illustrated in Figure 6.2. On the hori-

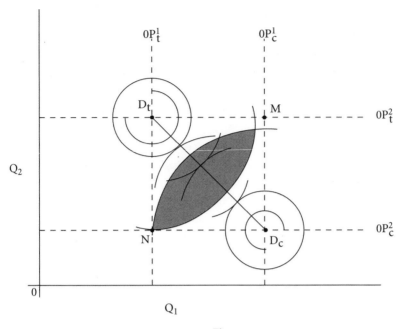

Figure 6.2

zontal axis, as before, we measure units of the first public good, Q_1, in this example, room temperature. On the vertical axis, we measure units of the second public good, Q_2, time for lights to go out. Each of the two persons will have some optimally preferred values for these two commonly shared items, some most desired combination. That for Tizio is indicated by D_t, that for Caio by D_c. These are peaks on the two preference or utility surfaces, assuming smoothness and continuity, and the functions can be represented by the standard indifference mappings. The set of curves enclosing D_t are indifference contours for Tizio; the set of curves enclosing D_c are indifference contours for Caio. The analysis that follows does not depend upon the particular locations of D_c and D_t.

By our assumption that the two variables are wholly independent in each utility function, the lines of optima enclose a rectangular area, shown here as $D_t M D_c N$. A single line of optima represents the locus of points at which an individual's set of indifference curves cut a horizontal or a vertical line. These lines are dotted in Figure 6.2, and are labeled with the $0P$s, the subscripts denoting the individuals, t and c, and the superscripts denoting the goods, Q_1

and Q_2. Hence, the line $0P_c^2$ depicts Caio's line of optima with respect to the good, Q_2. It indicates quantities of Q_2 that he would optimally prefer for all possible quantities of Q_1. By our assumption of independence, this is a horizontal line.

We propose now to examine the result of one particular decision rule. Consider the arbitrary but plausible rule that each one of the two men is given the authority to make one of the two decisions. Suppose, for illustration, that Tizio is allowed to decide what the temperature in the room shall be, while Caio is allowed to decide on the time for lights-out in the evening. The outcome will be that shown at N; if the two roles should be reversed, this outcome would be changed to M.

Once this rule is chosen, and the allocation of responsibility for each decision settled, the outcome at either N or M is an equilibrium one. So long as preferences do not change, this outcome will tend to be stable. In the simplified two-person model examined here, this rule for decision is, of course, only one from many that might be selected. It is singled out for some discussion because its analogue becomes important in the many-person model, the model which must be introduced when political choice is seriously analyzed. Majority voting rules produce results that are similar to those suggested here when all preferences exhibit single-peakedness and when issues are independently considered. In this situation, majority voting amounts to the delegation of decision-making power to one man, this man being, in each case, the member of the group whose preferences are median for the whole group.

It will be useful now to contrast the results reached under the arbitrary decision rule in the two-person case with those that might emerge when the two variables are simultaneously considered. When the two parties recognize that there are two variables to be settled, not one, and when they attempt to agree on a two-valued outcome, the range of possible results is dramatically narrowed to the positions along the contract locus D_tD_c. This is a contract locus of the ordinary sort, and *some* position on this locus will dominate any position off the locus, for *both* persons. Along the locus itself, no single point dominates any other point, for both persons. Note that this locus can be reached with an implicit unanimity rule for making final decision. The set of points along the locus are comparable in this sense with the set enclosed by the whole rectangle formed by intersecting lines of optima. *Without* joint consideration of the two variables, a solution anywhere in this rectangle becomes possible if common agreement is required for any change. *With* joint consideration, a solution anywhere on the locus becomes possible. The final position on the contract locus will remain indeterminate unless an arbitrary selection rule is adopted. In the absence of such a rule, the final outcome will depend on the skill and bargaining strength of the two parties.

Consider the position N, which we defined as one of equilibrium under the alternative decision rule examined. Assume that Tizio and Caio, finding themselves at N, now recognize that both variables may be simultaneously selected. Clearly, it is to the interest of both to reach agreement on moves from N in a generally northeasterly direction. Any move that lies within the lozenge that is shaded in Figure 6.2 will tend to be approved by both parties.

The construction demonstrates that, even in this model where both goods are purely public, simultaneous consideration allows the introduction of "economic" evaluation that is not possible under the alternative rule. The model is not one of exchange in the ordinary sense, since there is no transfer of goods between contracting parties. What they exchange here is agreement. Moving from N, in either a vertical or a horizontal direction, will make one of the two persons worse off. He is compensated for this worsening in his position, with respect to one of the two variables, by an improvement in his position with respect to the second variable.

It should be noted that this sort of exchange is not the same as vote trading, which we shall consider fully in a more inclusive model. The exchange depicted here is more closely described by "compromise" in a political-decision terminology. By simultaneously considering two variables rather than each variable separately, the possibility for mutual agreement between the parties is enhanced and there is less need for reliance on arbitrary decision rules. The results are more efficient than under any such rules, in that the preferences of the parties are more fully satisfied.

For analytical completeness, the two-person, two-good model should be modified to allow for complementarity and substitutability between the two purely public goods in one or both of the individual utility functions. One such geometrical construction, similar to Figure 6.2 but encompassing complementarity between the two goods in both utility functions, is shown in Figure 6.3. Note that the lines of optima for both parties now slope upward and to the right. If the arbitrary decision rule previously noted is chosen, with Tizio being granted authority to choose his preferred level of Q_1 and

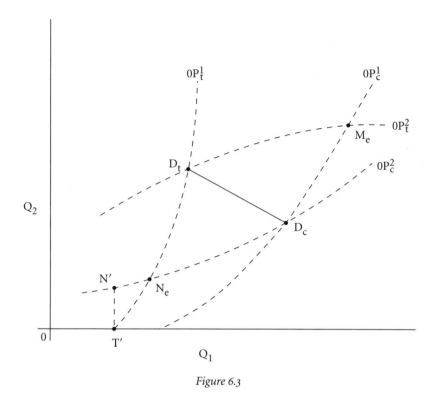

Figure 6.3

Caio being granted authority to choose his own preferred level of Q_2, an initial position at T' will be selected if Tizio acts first. Note, however, that this initial choice of Q_1 would no longer be stable. Finding himself at position N', after Caio has selected the indicated level of Q_2, Tizio would modify his initial choice. Caio would also shift his preferred position for Q_2. Equilibrium under this rule is finally attained, as before, at the intersection of the two lines of optima, shown at N_e in Figure 6.3. If the decision authority should be reversed for the two goods, the solution would shift to M_e.

As the construction of Figure 6.3 suggests, in this case when the two goods are complements in both utility functions and when the contract locus exhibits a negative slope, the delegation-of-decision rule is highly inefficient in comparison to a rule that allows simultaneous consideration of both goods and, hence, leads to some solution along the contract locus. If the two goods should be substitutes in both utility functions and the optimal positions should lie in the same relation to each other, the delegation-of-decision rule is, relatively, less inefficient than in the complementarity case. This conclusion is reversed if the contract locus exhibits a positive slope.

Geometrical elaboration of the argument to include the various relationships of complementarity and substitutability is omitted here for two reasons. The first is the obvious one of space; the second is the possible value that his own effort at geometrical construction can have for the student who desires to understand (and possibly to refute) the conclusions reached here, as well as those to be developed later in the chapter.

Three Persons, One Public Good

As the size of the group is expanded to include a third person, the analysis of agreement is necessarily modified. The first case, that in which all three must adjust to a single public good or "issue," can be covered briefly. To stay with our example, Tizio and Caio now have an additional roommate, Sempronio, who has a utility function that differs from either one of the other two. All three men must now adjust finally to the same quantity of the single variable, room temperature.

A three-person construction analogous to the two-person construction of Figure 6.1 is presented in Figure 6.4. The most preferred levels of tempera-

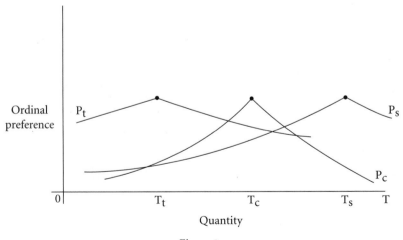

Figure 6.4

ture range from T_t to T_s, with T_c occupying a median position. We want to examine a single decision rule, that for simple-majority voting. So long as the ordinal preferences are single-peaked, as in Figure 6.1 or 6.4, and so long as individuals are free to suggest any quantity of the good to be chosen, the majority-rule solution will be T_c, the most preferred level for the median person with respect to this good. This can be easily seen by reference to Figure 6.4. Two out of three persons will approve all motions to increase quantities so long as these remain to the left of T_c; two out of three persons will approve all motions to decrease quantities, so long as these remain to the right of T_c. As a motion, T_c will defeat any alternative suggestions as to the quantity of the public good.

In the absence of any explicit decision rule, all three persons will agree only to limit the quantity to the range shown between T_t and T_s. Without a specific rule for choice other than general agreement, any point within this range becomes possible.

Three Persons, Two Public Goods

A more interesting, and more general, model emerges when we increase the number of public goods or issues to two, and extend the size of the interacting group to three. As we did with the two-person analysis, let us assume initially that the two goods are independent in each of the three utility functions. Figure 6.5 is a partial reproduction of Figure 6.2, with the addition of the third utility-function mapping. The most preferred combination for Sempronio is shown at D_s, and curves could be drawn enclosing this peak indicating his indifference contours (these are not drawn for economy reasons). The two lines of optima for Sempronio are shown as $0P_s^1$ and $0P_s^2$.

We now want to examine group decision-making when the two public goods, or issues, are considered separately. Under a rule of simple-majority voting, each issue will be decided as if it were the only one. The model previously analyzed for the single good is sufficiently explanatory. In terms of the construction of Figure 6.5, the solution will, in each case, lie somewhere on the *middle line of optima*. Considered separately, majority rule will produce decision on Q_1 somewhere along the line $0P_c^1$, and a decision on Q_2 somewhere along the line $0P_s^2$. The combination selected will be that shown at the *intersection of middle lines of optima*, indicated by V in the figure. By

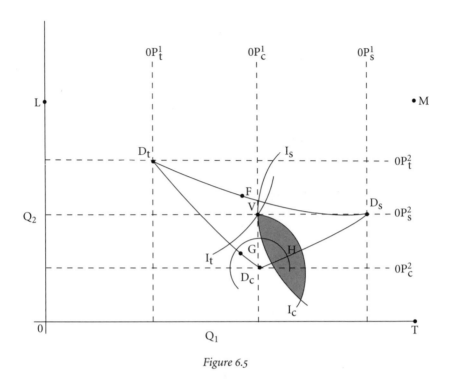

Figure 6.5

our restrictive assumption that the two goods are wholly independent in each utility function, the majority-rule choice for one good is not modified by the quantity of the other selected. This suggests that an initial majority-rule solution determining the quantity of one good will tend to be stable. The analysis here can be extended without difficulty to encompass any degree of complementarity or substitutability. After a series of votes, a combined solution is indicated at the appropriate intersection of middle lines of optima.

It will be useful to examine the independent majority-rule result, shown at V, somewhat more closely. Note that, as in the two-person case, this position is one of the extreme corners of the rectangle formed by lines of optima of the two decisive members of the group, Caio and Sempronio. As suggested earlier, this shows that majority voting, when preferences are single-peaked and when issues are considered separately, amounts to the delegation of choice on each issue to the person whose preferences are median for the group.

There are interesting differences between the two-person and three-person model in the comparison of results attained under the delegation-of-choice rule with issues considered separately and under the simultaneous consideration of both issues. In the two-person model, the alternate delegation of choice produced a result (at N in Figure 6.2) which was obviously inefficient in the Pareto sense once simultaneous consideration of both variables was recognized. *Both* members of the group found that their situations could be improved by shifting from N to a point on the contract locus. The three-person case is quite different. Majority rule does not delegate choice-making power arbitrarily; it delegates power to the person with the *median* preference. This insures that, given indifference contours of normal shape, the intersection of middle lines of optima, such as V in Figure 6.5, will lie *within* or upon the boundaries of the Pareto-optimal set of points, enclosed by the three contract loci. This set of points in the three-person case is equivalent to the contract locus in the two-person model.[4] The independent consideration of each issue, with simple-majority voting on each issue, will generate an outcome that will be Pareto-optimal, provided, of course, we remain within the model that denies the existence of a private-goods numeraire. Without such a numeraire, even potential side payments may not be brought into the discussion. The result will also tend to be an "equilibrium" one. So long as tastes do not change, and so long as the issues are not considered simultaneously, the rule will produce an outcome that will be stable over time.

If the two goods or issues are considered simultaneously, and simple-majority voting rules remain in effect, this equilibrium is rudely shattered. Note that, at V, both Caio and Sempronio can improve their own positions by suggesting combinations that lie within the shaded lozenge. They can, by active discussion of both issues simultaneously, move toward the contract lo-

---

4. The set of points that qualify as Pareto-optimal meet the same general conditions in the two-person and the three-person cases. Any point outside this set is dominated by at least one point in the set for all persons, and no point inside the set dominates any other point in the set for all persons. These conditions may be stated differently by reference to potential moves among points. From any nonoptimal point, there must exist at least one means of shifting to a point in the optimal set of points in such a way that at least one person is benefited and no one is harmed. In other words, it must be possible to shift from any nonoptimal point to some optimal point in a Pareto-optimal manner. Once a point within the Pareto set is attained, however, any shift must harm at least one person; no Pareto-optimal moves can be made.

cus, D_cD_s. Eventually, they will get to some position on this locus, say H. No further gains can be made by "exchanges" between these two persons, and, if they could be assured that Tizio will accept this result quietly, the position would be stable. However, note that, at H (as at V), gains-from-trade can be made as between Tizio and either one of the two other persons. Recognizing this, Tizio will propose a motion shifting the outcome to some combination, say that shown at G, and this will secure majority approval. Once having arrived at G, however, Sempronio may propose the combination F, which will, in turn, secure majority approval. At F, Caio may once again propose H, and this will, in its turn, win by a majority. When the two goods or issues are simultaneously included in motions, and when simple-majority voting rules remain in force, the outcome is likely to be a cycle among separate alternatives. This familiar phenomenon, that of a rotating or cycling majority outcome, need not take place only among positions on the boundaries of the Pareto-optimal area as in our example here. Cycles can occur as among combinations within the boundaries, but the latter set limits to the cyclical pattern if discrete "jumps" over these limits are ruled out. If, in each instance, the two members of the decisive majority coalition maximize the potential exploitation of the third, proposals or motions will tend to be those combinations along the contract loci.

The inconsistency represented by a cyclical majority is sometimes interpreted to be a serious limitation on the operability of a majority-voting rule, but, in terms of the model examined here, one fact must be noted. All points within the cycle are Pareto-optimal. Since it is not possible, without external criteria, to evaluate or weigh one Pareto-optimal position against the other (or even against certain nonoptimal positions), there is nothing that is necessarily inefficient about the cyclical majority pattern, except, of course, the inefficiencies introduced by the multiplicity of votes.

Let us now examine what might happen if there were no explicit decision rule in existence other than one requiring general agreement, and the situation is as depicted in Figure 6.5. If the two goods or issues are simultaneously considered, general agreement would produce a result within the Pareto-optimal area, bounded by the three contract loci. This is true almost by definition since we are ignoring, at this stage, costs of reaching agreement and also bargaining difficulties. No one result from within this area is any more plausible than any other in the general absence of a rule. If one of the three men assumes dictatorship, the outcome will, of course, be at one of the three optima. Many other possibilities might be examined, but space does not permit an elaboration of these.

Vote Trading and Intensities of Preference

The three-person, two-good model is helpful in understanding the elements of collective decision-making in larger groups. The geometrical exercises included in this chapter are selective, and only a skeletal group of configurations of utility functions and of relationships between goods in utility functions can be discussed in detail. The model previously used can, however, be extended to clarify an additional distinction, that between (1) simultaneous consideration of two goods or issues, and (2) explicit vote trading on single issues. To this point, we have examined the results predictable under simple-majority voting when the two decisions are made separately, and, secondly, the change that might be anticipated in these results when the two decisions are made simultaneously, when *combinations* are voted on as alternatives.

Neither of these institutions of group decision-making involves explicit vote trading. Simultaneous consideration of two variables allows agreement to be reached under exchange of a sort, but there is no explicit delegation of voting authority, no proxy transfer as it were. Such explicit trade, however, is a third possibility, and we may examine this within the three-person, two-good model.

The first point to be emphasized is that at least two goods or issues must be recognized to be present before vote trading can take place. This is an obvious point, especially to an economist, but it requires stress nonetheless because vote trading in an explicit sense requires a recognition of two issues but *separate* voting choices on each one of the two. It is not the same thing, therefore, as combining the issues and voting on a package, combination or bundle.

Under what circumstances would the three members of the group, as depicted in Figure 6.5, find it advantageous to trade votes explicitly? As we have seen, when the two decisions, on Q_1 and Q_2, are made separately, position V tends to be established by simple-majority voting. In this setting, Caio is the effective swingman, the decision maker, on Q_1; Sempronio is the effective decision maker on Q_2. Tizio is left out of account; he is an "extremist" on both issues; he desires more of Q_2 than anyone else and less of Q_1 than anyone else. Tizio might, in this situation, be quite happy to trade away his vote on either one of these two issues (he loses both in any case when no trades are made) in exchange for support of his own position on the second. Note, however, that as the utility functions are drawn in Figure 6.5, neither Caio nor Sempronio would be likely to agree to a trade offer from Tizio. Caio, for example, is already decisive with respect to Q_1; he would hardly give up this power of group choice in exchange for Tizio's vote on Q_2.

This no-trading result arises because, as we have mapped them onto Figure 6.5, the utility functions of all three potential traders exhibit relatively even strengths of preference as between the two issues. Geometrically, this means that the general shapes of the contours surrounding each optima are roughly similar. If the utility functions are different, and if at least one of the three persons should exhibit a relative intensity of preference for one of the two goods, explicit vote trading becomes a possibility even in this highly limited model.

To show this geometrically, a modified construction similar to Figure 6.5 is presented in Figure 6.6. For purposes of comparative analysis, the lines of optima are identical with those of the earlier figure, but the utility functions are now different. If the two decisions are made separately, the majority-rule outcome is, as before, that shown at V. Note, however, that both Tizio and Sempronio are better off at V' than at V. This preferred position, at V', which is the intersection between $0P_t^2$ and $0P_s^1$, can be attained by an explicit trade of votes. Recognizing that there are two decisions to be made, Tizio offers to support Sempronio's motion with respect to the amount of Q_1 in exchange for Sempronio's reciprocal support for Tizio's motion with respect to Q_2. As drawn in Figure 6.6, there are mutual gains from such trade. In the exchange, Sempronio gives up his power of effective decision over Q_2 because, relative to Tizio, he is more interested in Q_1.

Faced with this coalition between Tizio and Sempronio, there is nothing that Caio can do so long as the two issues are voted upon separately. He may, of course, denounce the exchange of votes as unethical, but he is powerless to offer terms more favorable to either member of the coalition, as the configurations drawn in Figure 6.6 indicate. He could offer his own decisive vote on Q_1 to Tizio, but the latter is relatively uninterested in this. The trading outcome represented at U is not likely to emerge. Or, alternatively, Caio might

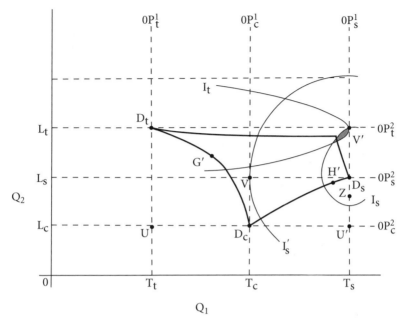

Figure 6.6

offer to trade with Sempronio, generating a possible trading outcome at U'. This would be a plausible result under slightly different configuration of Sempronio's utility function.

Trading outcomes will be located at the intersection of lines of optima so long as the exchanges take what might be called a proxy form. This means that the trade involves an agreement between two parties to exchange reciprocal support on undefined motions as to the quantities of specific goods. Under this restriction, outcomes, once attained, will tend to be reasonably stable. Trade may also be of a different sort and without this stability element. Faced with the outcome V', Caio may offer to Sempronio, not an exchange of proxies, but an exchange of specifically defined motions. He may agree to support Sempronio's motion for a quantity of Q_1 represented at T_s in exchange, not for his own optimally preferred quantity of Q_2, which would be L_c, but for a quantity measured by the distance T_sZ. Sempronio will find this trade advantageous since, at Z, his own position is clearly improved over that at V'. In turn, this may lead Tizio to make a further concession to Sempronio, and, by a series of exchanges on specific motions, Sempronio may actually approach his own optima for both variables. He is placed in this strategically favorable position here because Tizio is relatively interested in Q_2, not in Q_1, and Sempronio is an extremist with respect to Q_1, not Q_2.

Explicit vote trading of the proxy form tends to shift the majority-rule result outside the boundaries of the Pareto-optimal area enclosed by the three contract loci. To the extent that the trade departs from the proxy form and takes on that of exchanges of support on specific motions, the outcome shifts in the direction of the Pareto-optimal area, and, in one sense, the vote-trading equilibrium is attained at D_s, which is Pareto-optimal.

At either this outcome, D_s, or at V', or at any other outcome along the vertical from T_s, Caio is in a considerably worse position than at V, where no vote trading takes place. Rather than engage in a competition with Tizio for the favors of Sempronio, Caio might try to secure an institutional change that will allow both issues to be treated simultaneously rather than separately. If, faced with an outcome V', he can secure such a change, any offer of a combined package falling between V' and the contract locus within the shaded lozenge in Figure 6.6 will be approved by all three persons. However, once a position on the contract locus has been reached, Caio can proceed to form a new majority coalition with either of the other two persons, offering motions represented perhaps by either G' or H'.

One interesting configuration of utility functions is shown in Figure 6.7, which contains only the lines of optima. The same person exhibits median preferences for each good. If the two decisions are made separately, and if no vote trading takes place, he will reach his own optimal position. If, however, his two fellow citizens should differ from each other in relative intensity of preference as between the two goods, explicit vote trades may generate an outcome at either U or U' and the average man may be left out in the cold with neither of his median preferences honored. This model has considerable real-world suggestiveness, especially in the budgetary process. Congressmen from California are intensely interested in water-resource projects in the West; congressmen from West Virginia are interested in water-resource projects in Appalachia. Vote trades between these two may secure substantial appropriations for both, leaving the Iowa congressmen, who are mildly interested in both projects and with moderate preferences on each, without an effective voice in decisions.

Throughout this discussion of three-person models we have remained

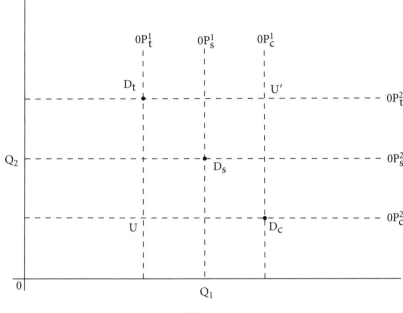

Figure 6.7

within the confines of the independence assumption. If the two goods are complements or substitutes in any of the individual's utility functions, the appropriate changes in results can be traced out with similar, but more complex, geometrical constructions. Basically, the conclusions reached under the model examined here are not modified. The exercises should have made clear that the outcome will depend not only on the relations between the two goods in individual utility functions, but, also, on the relationships among the separate utility functions of the separate persons, and on the institutions and rules for group decision-making. Until and unless these elements are specified, indeterminacies remain. Even when these are fully specified, outcomes may be unstable in the cyclical-majority sense.

Many Persons, Two Public Goods

So long as we remain in the two-good or two-issue model, the analysis can be extended without undue complexity to include any number of persons. Additional utility functions can be mapped onto the constructions developed in Figures 6.2, 6.5, 6.6 and 6.7. Consider a five-man group, as illustrated in Figure 6.8. The positions D_1 through D_5 are the optimally preferred combinations. For purposes of economy, indifference contours surrounding each peak are not drawn.

When the two issues are separately considered, and simple-majority voting is the decision rule, the solution remains that shown by the intersection between middle lines of optima, position V. The contract loci connecting the separate positions of optima are drawn in Figure 6.8. For obvious reasons these take on a somewhat reduced significance in all models that include more than three persons. No longer will agreement between two persons alone constitute a majority. All points along or within the boundaries of the area enclosed by the contract loci are not, therefore, possible majority-rule outcomes when the two goods are simultaneously considered, as was the case with the three-person group. This outside boundary encloses, as before, the Pareto-optimal set of positions. Under a rule of unanimity, some position

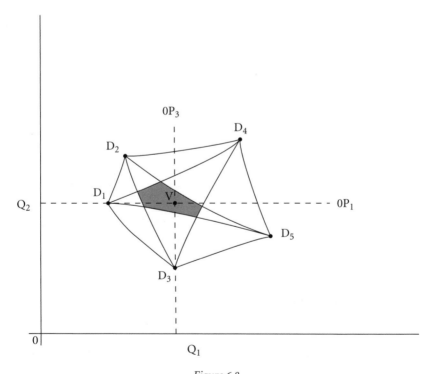

Figure 6.8

within or on the boundaries of this area would be attained. With majority rule, however, simultaneous consideration of both issues will produce solutions contained within a subset of this larger Pareto-optimal set. Under specific assumptions about the shapes of the indifference contours, assumptions that are within the normal constraints of convexity and continuity, the "majority-rule area" can be isolated. Within this area, the voting process will produce cyclical results with constantly changing coalitions. Under plausible assumptions about the range of variation in alternatives presented for the pairwise voting comparisons, this area may approximate that of the shaded five-sided inner figure. The details of analysis need not concern us here. The main point is that the majority-rule set is now a subset of the Paretian set, an important difference between all models with more than three persons and the three-person model.

As the number of persons in the interacting group expands, the Pareto-optimal set of positions or points also expands, as the construction indicates, but the majority-rule set as a proportion of the Pareto-optimal set is reduced in size. This suggests that even in large groups, although the problem of cyclical majorities will remain, the set of alternative combinations over which results will cycle tends to become smaller and smaller, in some sense relative to the total possible range of decisions. With very large groups, the discrete area over which majority outcomes may cycle may substantially disappear. Wide and discrete shifts in outcomes are not likely to emerge under the operation of simple-majority voting unless institutional barriers prevent the offering of compromise motions. For extreme shifts to occur, the alternatives must be largely restricted to those that are themselves extreme, relative to the particular configuration of preferences among members of the group.

Vote trading may, of course, take place in such many-person models, especially if the number of parties is not overwhelmingly large. Given specific preference configurations among subgroups, results akin to those developed in connection with the three-person model can emerge. The group of individuals whose preferences dictate an extreme position with respect to one of the two variables along with a relative indifference as to the other variable and a decisive median position with respect to the latter is advantageously placed for strategic trading. Interesting examples can be developed by considering *n*-persons subdivided broadly into a relatively small number of pressure groups.

Many Persons, Many Public Goods

The most general of all possible models is one in which the interacting group contains a large number of persons and where there are many goods, each one of which is purely public. The two-dimensional confines of plane geometry are no longer helpful, even in the three-person, three-good case. Pictures of three-dimensional space may be attempted, and three-dimensional constructions are helpful in classroom presentation. But even the standard economists' calculus provides little assistance here, since the required conditions for equilibrium, under any rule for decision, cannot readily be stated.

We do not propose to examine this model in detail; references in the appendix are provided for those whose intellectual curiosity prompts them to follow up the suggestions made. The summary comments will be limited to specific relationships that are more or less intuitive.

As the size of the group expands, the Pareto-optimal set of positions also expands, but the majority-rule set contracts, relative to the Paretian set. This has already been shown with reference to comparisons between the three-person and five-person models when only two goods are considered. The relationship holds generally as the number of variables, goods or issues, is increased.

On the other hand, as the number of goods or issues increases, the Pareto-optimal set of positions tends to contract in a relative sense. This second relationship has not been discussed, but it can be shown in the three-person model as the number of goods increases from one to two. Refer to Figure 6.4. The possible range of solutions on the single variable Q_1 extends from 0 to T. The Pareto-optimal set of positions, that set from which one position would be attained under a rule of unanimity, includes all positions along the spectrum ranging from T_t through T_s. If we can assume that positions are discrete and that possible outcomes are uniformly measured, the Pareto-optimal set clearly makes up more than one-half of the total set of possible outcomes. Now, by comparison, refer to Figure 6.5, when a second dimension has been added. The possible solutions for the variable, Q_2, are shown by the range $0L$. Conceptually, therefore, all possible combinations of Q_1 and Q_2 are contained in the rectangle $0LMT$. If we again assume discreteness and uniformity over the whole space, it is clear that the set of positions or outcomes enclosed by the contract loci, the Pareto-optimal set, makes up considerably less than one-half the total set of prospects. Again this relationship is a general one, and as the number of goods is increased, the solution set, given any decision rule, tends to contract, relative to the total set of attainable alternatives.

There is a commonsense basis for this second relationship. As the number of goods expands, even if all of these are purely public in the sense that all persons must adjust to the same quantity, individual expressions of preference can be more fully reflected, at least for that subset of persons who are in the decisive coalition as determined by the decision rule in being. Each member of the coalition has in hand, so to speak, a more varied set of counters and this allows him to reach accord with other members more readily and at less cost. The economic analogue, which must be used with caution, is a genuine barter system of exchange. In the absence of a money commodity, an agreed-on numeraire, each potential seller must seek out a buyer for the particular good he has to offer and *vice versa*. It seems clear that the larger the number of goods in his possession the more fully can an individual secure that final set of goods dictated by his utility function as the most desirable. The advice for caution in the use of this analogy lies in the fact that, with barter in private goods, all exchanges are bilateral. In the public-goods model, even when there are many separate goods, individuals cannot exchange or transfer goods directly. Exchange cannot be bilateral in the standard sense. Agreements can be exchanged, or votes traded, but, in either case, the trading behavior will affect others who are not direct parties to the exchange. There remains an inherent externality in any group-choice situation that may be absent from private-goods trading.

As stated at the outset, the analytical exercises presented in this chapter are aimed at partially bridging the gap between the economic theory of public goods, explored in Chapters 1 through 5, and the theory of political or collective choice, to be examined more thoroughly in subsequent chapters. Little if any of the material discussed in this book has yet attained the status of orthodoxy or received doctrine, and this applies with special force to the nonnumeraire models considered in this chapter. Only a handful of scholars has worked with such models. The whole analysis remains in its infancy.

Bibliographical Appendix

The theory of committees and elections was pioneered by Duncan Black, and was exhaustively analyzed in his book [*The Theory of Committees and*

Elections (Cambridge: Cambridge University Press, 1958)]. This provides the background for all models containing only the single public good or issue. As developed by Black and others, the theory does not explicitly refer to "public goods," but to issues, motions or candidates in an election when only one alternative is to be chosen. It is also in this context that the discussion of the "paradox of voting," or cyclical majorities, has taken place. The now-classic work on this, in addition to Black's, is Kenneth J. Arrow's book [*Social Choice and Individual Values* (New York: John Wiley and Sons, 1951; Revised edition, 1963)].

The extension of the models to two goods, again discussed in terms of issues, was initially contained in a much-neglected small book by Duncan Black and R. A. Newing [*Committee Decisions with Complementary Valuation* (London: William Hodge, 1951)]. This book contains extremely interesting geometrical exercises and illustrations, some of which are closely akin to those presented in parts of Chapter 6.

Otto A. Davis and Melvin Hinich have provided a formal mathematical treatment of the behavioral strategy of candidates and parties seeking election as the relevant variables are extended from one to many ["A Mathematical Model of Policy Formation in a Democratic Society," in *Mathematical Applications in Political Science, II,* edited by Joseph L. Bernd (Dallas: Southern Methodist University Press, 1966); "Some Results Related to a Mathematical Model of Policy Formation in a Democratic Society" (Mimeographed, Carnegie Institute of Technology, May 1966)].

In the context of formal welfare economics, Ragnar Frisch's paper ["On Welfare Theory and Pareto Regions," *International Economic Papers,* No. 9 (London: Macmillan, 1959), pp. 39–92] develops the two-good case exhaustively and extends the analysis to many dimensions.

Building on the work of both Black and Frisch, Charles Plott completed the most rigorous statement of the necessary conditions for equilibrium under alternative decision rules in the many-persons, many-goods model [*Generalized Equilibrium Conditions Under Alternative Exchange Institutions,* Research Monograph No. 9 (Charlottesville: Thomas Jefferson Center for Political Economy, University of Virginia, December 1964)].

The analysis of the section which discusses the model containing many persons and two public goods has been exhaustively treated by Gordon Tullock ["The General Irrelevance of the General Impossibility Theorem," *Quar-*

terly Journal of Economics, LXXXI (May 1967), 256–70]. He examines this model in particular relation to Arrow's discussion.

My own analysis of the material in Chapter 6 owes much to many discussions, extending over several years, with Duncan Black, Charles Plott and Gordon Tullock. Should they be willing to accept my interpretations, I should be happy to list them all, informally, as joint authors.

7. The Publicness
of Political Decisions

Introduction

Individuals demand certain goods and services that they supply publicly through political rather than market organization. These goods enter as arguments in individual utility functions, and a theory of demand can be derived. The modern theory of public goods has been largely devoted to such derivation. If interpreted properly, this theory provides predictive hypotheses concerning the outcomes of collective decision processes under certain highly restrictive assumptions. At the same time and in a more familiar context, the theory provides allocative or efficiency norms for the provision of these goods and services. In either usage, the theory applies to *any* goods and services that are, for any reason, organized publicly. The technical characteristics of goods may and should influence the decisions on the appropriate organization of supply. This will be discussed more fully in Chapter 9. But the theory, as such, is appropriate to *public organization* for any good or service.

This "publicness" in the organization of supply requires further discussion. To the extent that decisions are made politically, regardless of their specific content, there are "public-goods" elements present. It is in this context that the theoretical exercises of Chapter 6 provide a useful bridge between the analysis of private demand and that of "public supply." In a world without a private-good numeraire, all decisions are necessarily public, whether these be concerned with the supply of particular goods or with rules that govern behavior. For this reason, in Chapter 6, quantities of public goods, issues and even candidates for elective office were often used interchangeably as the objects of collective choice; deliberate ambiguity was employed as a means of stressing the identity of the analysis in each case.

Public goods and private goods are indistinguishable as they enter individual utility functions. Individuals want different things. With privately supplied goods, market exchange facilitates individual adjustments to preferred quantities, within limits imposed by resource constraints, in total and in individually divisible shares. The outcome of a private-goods trade is a changed allocation or distribution of commodities among individual traders. The situation is quite different with public goods. The outcome of "exchange," through some collective decision rule, is "agreement" on the same quantity of good, to be shared by all traders and *commonly* consumed. There is no individual quantity adjustment. Individual adjustments must be made in "prices," not in quantities, if the outcomes are to be classified as efficient in the standard sense.

Earlier chapters have shown that the required differentiation in the structure of prices for public goods may emerge as a result of "trades" among individuals when the number in the trading process remains small. Adjustments in the cost-shares measured in money, a perfectly divisible numeraire, will take place until agreement is reached on a quantity of the common good. When the number of persons is large, the autonomous emergence of such a "pricing" pattern cannot be predicted. In the real world where public goods are shared by large numbers of persons, the "pricing structure" must be agreed on in much the same manner as the quantity of good to be provided. This aspect of public-goods theory has been relatively neglected, perhaps largely because the emphasis has been placed on the derivation of efficiency norms rather than on the processes of collective agreement. In the strictly formal sense, the satisfaction of the necessary conditions for efficiency or optimality implies the presence of a structure of marginal prices. When this level of formalism is dropped and the process of reaching agreement among persons is analyzed, the problem becomes two-dimensional at best. Agreement must be reached on the quantity of the public goods to be supplied and on the sharing of the cost, both in total and at the margin, among separate members of the group.

To an individual, these are clearly related decisions. The amount of any public good that he will prefer will depend on the share in its cost that he individually must bear. Most persons would prefer a larger quantity the lower their own share in the payment. This is a simple application of the first law of demand which, when combined with commonality in consumption, provides the basis for the free-rider problem already discussed in Chapter 5. It is misleading, however, in the large-number model to attempt to derive a structure of individual shares from an analysis of offers and counter-offers. Conceptually, this sort of analysis is possible, because individuals can make such offers differentially in the private-goods or money numeraire, which is fully divisible among persons, but it is relevant only when very small numbers are involved. And, in these cases, strategic elements of behavior tend to be unduly stressed. A different analytical framework is required for large-number settings.

At one level of analysis, there seems nothing public about the individual's own tax-share. Different individuals may be subjected to different tax-prices; there seems to be no common sharing in the ordinary sense. However, this approach overlooks the necessary publicness of the decision over the sharing of public-goods cost among persons. Individuals can express their preferences, through some voting scheme, only on tax-sharing *schemes* or *structures*. They can vote on a whole set of tax-prices or tax-shares, total and marginal, and this set necessarily includes not only their own liability but those for all other members of the group. It is impossible for an individual to "offer" his own desired payment, independent of payments to be made by all others. It is in this sense that alternative sharing schemes are "purely public." Each person must adjust his own behavior to the *same* scheme of payment; the fact that this is chosen and enforced politically insures its publicness, despite the fact that individual payments are to be made in a fully divisible numeraire. The scheme, or schemes when alternatives are considered, may contain widely differing shares for different persons. Descriptively, any alternative here is a vector with characteristics of individual tax shares as components.

The General Nature of Tax-Sharing Schemes

As the small-number trading models as well as the more formal mathematical ones suggest, "price" differentials among separate demanders of public goods must reflect differentials in preferences, even down to the individual level, if the necessary conditions for optimality are to be satisfied. In large-number situations appropriate to real-world fiscal decisions, the fine discrimination dictated by such conditions can hardly be achieved. Not only would great difficulties be encountered in reaching agreement, but the large number of sharing possibilities cannot even be considered. Alternatives presented for political decision must be severely limited. This suggests that, almost necessarily, the sharing arrangements presented will reflect objectively determinate criteria for "price differentials." At best, therefore, alternative tax-sharing vectors among which choice is possible will subdivide individuals into broad groups, classified not in terms of their privately expressed public-goods preferences but in terms of general characteristics that are presumably related to such preferences in some representative or average sense. *General* criteria will be employed to establish classificatory systems, and the satisfaction of the necessary conditions for efficiency in public-goods supply will be approached only to the extent that actual preferences of individuals are arrayed roughly in accord with these general criteria.

One common and almost universally used general classification relies on the relative economic positions of individuals (families) as defined by appropriate income-wealth measures. Personal income or wealth is taken as an externally selected criterion for imposing relative tax-shares, and the more sophisticated fiscal theorists have supported this procedure on the ground that this criterion does correspond roughly to relative demands for public goods. This relationship is likely to hold only for general-benefit goods, and only to the extent that they exhibit positive income elasticities of demand. This seems to be one general presumption underlying modern fiscal structures.

Any general classification in which tax liabilities are related to variables that individuals can control creates difficulties. Individuals will attempt to reduce their relative shares in the costs of public goods by shifting their position as defined by the basis of the sharing scheme. Such shifting can take place only within limits, however, and the underlying classification in accordance with income-wealth criteria is also presumed to remain relevant. Given a general income-wealth criterion, more explicit definition of the relative shares will depend on the predicted shifts in individual behavior, and, this aside, specific allocation of shares will arouse disagreement, but this aspect of the problem need not be discussed at this point.

Within an income-wealth classification and given some specific rate structure, an individual's tax-share will finally be determined, not by his own particular demand for or evaluation of the public good (or public-goods bundles) but by his position in the private economy after he has made his tax-base adjustments. He is never in a position where he can react to the "offers" of others in any direct sense. He cannot express his public-goods preferences explicitly. He can, however, express these indirectly through the political process. He can, directly or through his participation (or nonparticipation) in electing representatives, approve or disapprove various tax-share vectors and various proposals for public-spending programs. Preferring high levels of public-goods supply, he will vote for larger spending projects and, perhaps, for tax-sharing arrangements that place higher shares on his own income-wealth class. As the analysis below will indicate, however, there is much less likelihood that individuals will positively approve increases in their own tax-shares.

A Simplified Two-Person Model

To analyze collective agreement on both public-goods quantity and tax-sharing arrangements, it will once again be helpful to resort to the simple two-person model because much of the analysis carries over into the relevant many-person models. We want to examine the behavior of two persons, High and Low, as they adjust to two public variables: first, the quantity of public goods, and, secondly, the specific tax-sharing scheme to finance this quantity. For simplicity in presentation, we shall assume initially that all tax-sharing alternatives to be considered embody marginal tax-prices to individual taxpayers that are constant over quantity.

The individuals are assumed to be independently classified by their relative economic positions. High stands high by income-wealth criteria and Low stands low. The single public good is assumed to be beneficial to both and to have a positive income elasticity of demand for both.

The situation can be shown in Figure 7.1, which is related to the constructions introduced in Chapter 6. The quantity of the public good is shown along the horizontal axis, and is measured in dollars worth of outlay. This allows us to incorporate the costs of the good in this variable. We assume that the unit cost of the good is fixed. Tax-share vectors are arrayed along the vertical axis. To accomplish this, some index must be selected. Given the various simplifications imposed on this model, the index can be a relatively

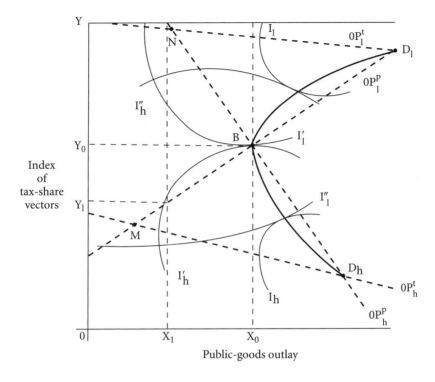

Figure 7.1

simple one measuring "share progressivity" in the tax structure. At the origin, we locate that tax-sharing scheme which assigns to Low 100 per cent of the total cost of the public good, regardless of the amount to be financed. At *Y,* the other extreme, we locate the tax-sharing plan that assigns 100 per cent of the cost of the public good to High, regardless of the amount to be financed. All possible sharing schemes are arrayed between these limits.

The preferences of the two individuals can be mapped onto Figure 7.1 in the standard fashion. Low's most desired combination is likely to be located at some point, D_l, where there is a large quantity of the good supplied but where this is almost wholly financed by taxes levied on High. The most preferred combination for High is less predictable, but presumably at some point, D_h, he will desire a relatively large quantity of the public good that is financed through a tax-sharing scheme that keeps his own share relatively low. The probable presence of certain equity considerations in High's utility function insures that his optimally preferred position will lie somewhere above the horizontal axis.

Following the construction of Chapter 6, lines of optima may be drawn in Figure 7.1. The shapes of these under our set of assumptions seem predictable. Low's line of public-goods optima will take the general shape shown by $0P_l^p$. This indicates the amount of public good which Low will optimally prefer at all possible tax-share arrangements arrayed in accordance with the share progressivity index. Clearly, this line will be positively sloped, indicating that Low will desire a larger quantity of the public good as his own share in the cost is reduced and High's share increased. It also seems reasonable to expect that this line of optima for Low will have some positive intercept on the vertical axis. This indicates that, at some level of the tax-share index, he will prefer to forego completely the benefits of the public good because his own payment becomes too large, and competing demands on his resources make him unwilling to pay for the public good at these levels of taxation.

High's comparable public-goods line of optima will tend to be negatively sloped, but the absolute value of the slope will perhaps be somewhat higher than that for Low. The line of optima may not intersect the vertical axis below Y, suggesting that High may be willing to finance a certain quantity of the good even if he is forced to bear the full costs. As his cost-shares fall below this level, he will prefer larger amounts of the good, but, as the absolute slope indicates, he will be less sensitive than Low to his share in the payment.

Lines of tax-share optima can also be derived from the indifference contours and these are drawn in as $0P_l^t$ and $0P_h^t$ on Figure 7.1. Low will clearly prefer a tax-sharing scheme that will at all levels of provision impose the predominant share of the cost on High. High may accept larger shares of public-goods costs at lower budgetary levels than at higher ones. To indicate this possibility his line of tax-share optima is drawn with a slight downslope.

If one of the two persons should be assigned the decision authority over tax shares and the other over public-goods quantity, the resulting equilibrium would be either at M or at N. In either case, the result would be extremely inefficient and would allow for a relatively small total outlay.

Significant differences are to be noted in the relative positions of the two lines of optima in each case, and this is important for the theory of collective agreement. Note that the lines of optima for the two persons, with respect to the preferred quantities of public goods, intersect at B. There is no comparable intersection of the tax-share lines of optima. At the tax-sharing scheme, Y_0, both parties will agree on a most desired public outlay. This defines a Pareto-optimal solution, given the limitations imposed on this model. Note that, at B, the public-goods lines of optima intersect and also cut the contract locus. All points on this locus are, of course, Pareto-optimal in the larger sense. These include the extreme limits, D_h and D_l, one of which would prevail should all decision power be vested in one man. The position shown at B, however, seems to embody "reasonableness" characteristics for a solution not possessed by other positions on the locus. If the two persons commence at the origin, where none of the public good is being provided, B seems to be a reasonable outcome of negotiations on both variables, since it is the maximum public-goods quantity upon which the two persons can reach agreement given a unique tax-sharing scheme. This scheme reflects the precise structure of "price differentials" to bring public-goods preferences into agreement.

Note that at B, the lines of tax-share optima remain widely separated. There is no comparable agreement on this variable subject to collective choice. The reason is that this variable is almost purely distributional; an increase in one person's tax-share reduces that of the other. At any level of outlay, either person would prefer to secure that outlay at a lower rather than at a higher cost to himself.

It is interesting to examine Wicksell's unanimity proposals within this framework. He suggested that for each expenditure proposal advanced, an array of tax-sharing schemes should be considered, and unless at least one such scheme could secure unanimous approval the expenditure should not be made. Suppose that, in terms of Figure 7.1, an initial proposal is made to spend an amount X_1 on the public good. Tax-sharing schemes are presented along with this spending proposal. In this context, any tax-sharing scheme falling between Y_1 and Y may be approved by both parties, ignoring purely strategic behavior. For an amount of spending, X_1, High would, if necessary, finance the whole cost. Similarly, Low would, if necessary, pay a major share as indicated in the scheme at Y_1. Agreement becomes possible, on some tax-sharing arrangement *and* on the spending proposal, anywhere between these limits. Having adopted this initial spending proposal, suppose that a further proposal is made in the second round to expand the level of outlay incrementally. Agreement remains possible, with many alternative sharing schemes on such increments, but the multiplicity of possible arrangements diminishes rapidly as X_0 is approached. At the margin, at X_0, only one sharing scheme can command the approval of both parties, that shown by Y_0. For all proposals to expand spending beyond X_0, no sharing scheme will command the approval of both parties.

The position shown at B is, therefore, the uniquely determinate Wicksellian solution to the problem of public-goods allocation and tax-sharing, given the restrictions of our model. These restrictions include constant marginal tax-shares over quantity. This particular restriction can be relaxed; the construction remains useful, but only if income-effect feedbacks on individual preferences are neglected. In this case, the solution is determinate in terms of *marginal* tax-shares and public-goods outlay. Any number of sharing schemes over inframarginal units becomes possible. If income-effects are taken into consideration, no such determinacy can be represented diagrammatically.

It may also be useful to compare, in a general way, these results with those suggested in the familiar set of efficiency norms advanced by Samuelson. These are stated as marginal conditions that must be satisfied for optimality and do not include explicit reference to total conditions. A uniquely determinate result is attained only by resort to an externally derived "social welfare function" which does, of course, specify the final distribution of "welfare." Almost by definition, the necessary marginal conditions are satisfied at any point on the contract locus between D_h and D_l in Figure 7.1. Samuelson then calls upon the social welfare function to select from among these points. He does not deal with the processes of reaching agreement on specific outcomes.

Extension to Three-Person Models

Only within two-person limits is the analysis of collective agreement on the two fiscal variables wholly free of complexities which would tend to obscure the essential elements under discussion if introduced too early. These complexities arise in three-person models and are compounded as the analysis is extended to larger groups.

As shown in the exercises of Chapter 6, no problem arises in adding utility-function mappings for other persons onto a construction similar to Figure

7.1, *provided* that the variables are treated as purely collective or public goods. We have argued above that all individuals must adjust to a common tax-sharing arrangement or tax structure and that, despite the divisibility of individual tax-shares, these structures can best be analyzed as if they are public goods (or public bads). This creates no problems in a purely formal sense, but serious difficulties arise in any analysis of a group decision process.

These stem from attempts to array tax-share vectors on the vertical axis in such a way that, as between this variable and the public-goods variable measured along the horizontal axis, individual preference mappings exhibit the standard properties of convexity. This task of arraying tax-share vectors is greatly simplified in the two-person case. Here individual shares in cost must be strictly related, one to the other. Since the total must sum to unity, an increase in the share of one person can only mean a decrease, *pari passu*, in the share of the second. The utility functions of both persons defined on the two variables, public-goods outlay and an index of tax-share vectors, can be expected to exhibit the standard properties.

With three persons, no such one-to-one correspondence among individual shares can exist; an increase in the tax-share for one person may be accompanied by a decrease in the share of *either one* or *both* of the other two persons. For any one person, it is possible to array tax-share vectors in such a way that a utility mapping will exhibit convexity. But it will not be possible, in the general case, that this same index will allow for convexity in the mappings for all three persons.

To resolve this difficulty let us first place one additional restriction on the set of tax-sharing arrangements to be considered. Plausibly, we impose the requirement that cost-shares shall not be related inversely to the external criterion that is used to classify persons or groups. If income is used here, this restriction suggests only that those persons with lower incomes shall not be required to contribute cost-shares higher than persons standing above them on the independent income scale, regardless of relative preferences for public goods. In any real-world context, no tax-sharing arrangement is likely to violate this additional restriction, although, in a formal sense, particular configurations of public-goods preferences may make adherence to this restriction produce inefficient results *per se*. These latter possibilities have, however, already been ruled out by our earlier assumption that for each person there is a positive income elasticity of demand for the public good. The practical effect of this restriction is that the alternative standing lowest on the tax-vector index is defined by equal sharing among all persons in the group.

(a) Symmetry with respect
to median income

With this restriction, we can now examine the three-person model first under an extremely helpful, and not implausible, simplifying assumption that further limits the set of tax-sharing arrangements to be considered as alternatives. We assume that the share of the median-income person in the three-person group shall remain unchanged over all possible arrangements. In an earlier work, I have referred to this characteristic as symmetry with respect to the median-income person. An arithmetical example will clarify the precise meaning here. As suggested, the lowest point on the index will represent a vector indicating equal tax-shares, or vector ($\frac{1}{3}$, $\frac{1}{3}$, $\frac{1}{3}$). As we move up the index or scale, the share of the low-income man decreases and the share of the high-income man increases, but the share of the median man remains unchanged at one-third. The highest point on the index is represented by the vector (0, $\frac{1}{3}$, $\frac{2}{3}$). This simplification, in effect, converts the three-person model into the two-person one.

Geometrical representation is in Figure 7.2. The situations of two of the three persons, Low and High, are substantially identical with those in Figure 7.1. For the third man, Median, only one of the two dimensions is intensively relevant. Since he will, under our assumption, pay one-third of the cost of the public good, regardless of the distribution of the remaining two-thirds among his two colleagues, he will tend to prefer approximately the same level of public-goods outlay at all tax-sharing schemes. If we allow him to exhibit some concern for distributional consequences, we may locate his most preferred single combination at D_m, somewhat nearer to the upper bound of the tax-vector set than to the lower. At best, however, we should expect his indifference contours to be elongated, and his public-goods line of optima to be steep, as shown by $0P_m^p$. If Median is concerned exclusively with his own share, there will be no tax-share line of optima, but, again, if we allow for some distributional motivation, this line may lie roughly as shown by $0P_m^t$ in Figure 7.2.

With this setting, what can be predicted to emerge as a result of collective-

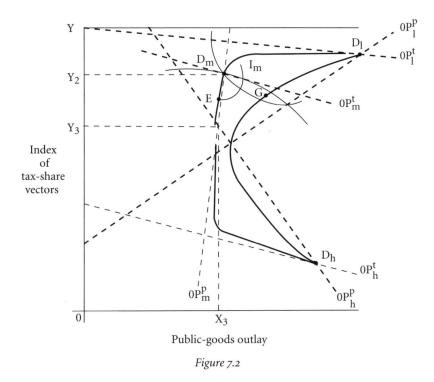

Figure 7.2

choice processes? The contract surface takes the shape enclosed by the heavy solid lines of Figure 7.2. Let us initially consider the predicted outcome when the two variables are decided upon separately and by simple-majority voting rules. As the analysis of Chapter 6 showed, the solution in this case is given by the intersection of middle lines of optima, shown at D_m. In the configuration as drawn, this process of decision effectively allows Median to dictate the community outcome for both variables. He attains his "peak" level of preference. At this solution, there will be widespread disagreement concerning the most preferred public-goods outlay. With a tax-sharing scheme presented at Y_2, High will prefer a much smaller budget, while Low will prefer a much larger one. Wicksellian unanimity is far from being achieved in the shift to this solution.

Consider now a modification in the decision rules that allows for simultaneous consideration of both variables, again under simple-majority voting rules. Suppose that the solution at D_m has been provisionally stabilized and that a coalition between High and Low forms and proposes a shift to G. Clearly, both men will benefit, Low accepting a somewhat larger share in cost in exchange for High's agreement for an expanded public-goods outlay. This position, at G, will not, of course, be majority-stable. Cyclical shifts can take place within and upon the bounds of the contract surface. Certain plausible restrictions can be placed on such moves in the particular configuration of Figure 7.2. Median is primarily if not exclusively interested in shifting horizontally; he is relatively indifferent as between vertical alternatives, at any level. Accordingly, High is much more likely to succeed in forming a new coalition with Median to organize shifts away from G. If he does so, some shift to a new position, say E, will take place. This will be somewhat closer to a Wicksellian solution in that the disagreement over public-goods quantity will be substantially less intense at this point than at D_m or at G. However, this position, E, is not majority-stable either, and further shifts can be made.

A similar analysis could, of course, be carried out no matter where the lines of optima should be located for Median with respect to those for the other two persons.

The construction suggests that majority-decision rules, whether these involve separate consideration of issues or simultaneous consideration, will not produce solutions that will be accepted by all parties, save in some constitutional sense of acquiescence. The result produced by majority voting may, as in the above examples, qualify as a Pareto-optimal position once it is attained, but it cannot be *attained Pareto-optimally*. Distributional elements will necessarily be present in the decision process. These are, of course, likely to be omnipresent in real-world fiscal choices and to this extent the model is highly realistic, but it will be useful to examine the Wicksellian unanimity rule as an alternative in this particular submodel.

As drawn, there is no Wicksellian solution in the strictly marginal sense as discussed in connection with Figure 7.1. For public-goods outlay proposals up to X_3, there are many tax-sharing schemes that will be accepted. Beyond X_3, disagreement appears; Median objects to further outlay, and given the limits on the tax-sharing vectors imposed by our symmetry assumption, no further moves can be made with general consent. A proximate Wicksellian solution is, therefore, attainable at an outlay, X_3, and a tax-sharing scheme, Y_3.

(b) Lexicographic ordering

Symmetry in share progressivity with respect to median income is unduly restrictive. Some attempt must be made to construct an index of tax-share vectors without this crutch. We propose to construct an index that will reflect a lexicographic ordering of the vectors. As before, we retain the restriction that the lowest vector on the scale will be that which indicates equal sharing among all members of the community. Above this, we first array all possible vectors in subsets classified Low's share, in ascending order as this share falls. The vectors in each of these subsets will represent different means of residual sharing between Median and High. Within each of these subsets, we then array vectors in ascending order as Median's share falls. This type of ordering can be extended to any number of persons and can include all possible tax-sharing schemes, given the initial restrictions imposed on all of the models.

An arithmetical illustration of this ordering will be helpful. Assume that a possible set of tax-share vectors to be ordered is:

(.1, .3, .6)   (.2, .4, .4)   (.1, .2, .7)   (.1, .4, .5)   (.2, .3, .5)   (.1, .1, .8)
(.2, .2, .6)

Arraying these along a vertical scale we get:

g (.1, .1, .8)
f (.1, .2, .7)
e (.1, .3, .6)
d (.1, .4, .5)
c (.2, .2, .6)
b (.2, .3, .5)
a (.2, .4, .4)

This procedure generates a systematic ordering of all possible vectors, but it does not eliminate the convexity problem. Consider the limited array above. Note that Median pays a larger tax-share in both d and e than he does in c, while High pays a lower tax-share in d than he does in c. For both Median and High, preference mappings will exhibit nonconvexity.

Figure 7.3 depicts the likely pattern of indifference contours for High. His optimally preferred combination is shown at D_h, located roughly in the same position as before. Note, however, that local peaks will occur at D', D'', and D'''. As abrupt shifts are made from one subset to another, High's utility is increased, locally, despite the general decline in his utility as his position is moved northwestward. For example, at D'', because of the shift of subset, he may be brought suddenly back to a level of utility equal to that attained on the contour I'. The public-goods line of optima for High will roughly follow the pattern shown by the dotted line on Figure 7.3. This lies within an area confined by the two solid lines, and the width of this area progressively widens as we move vertically up the figure. This is because of the greater range of distributional splits between Median and High as Low's share is reduced.

Figure 7.4 depicts, in similar way, the utility mapping for Median. As shifts are made between subsets classified by Low's share, Median will also confront "cliffs," and his preference surface will exhibit local peaks at D', D'', and D'''. Because of the ordering scheme used, these local cliffs will be facing opposite to those of High. This can be noted in the arithmetical array. As a shift

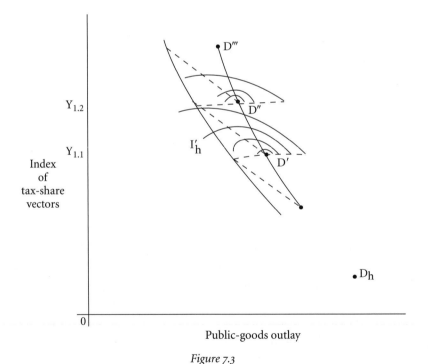

Public-goods outlay

Figure 7.3

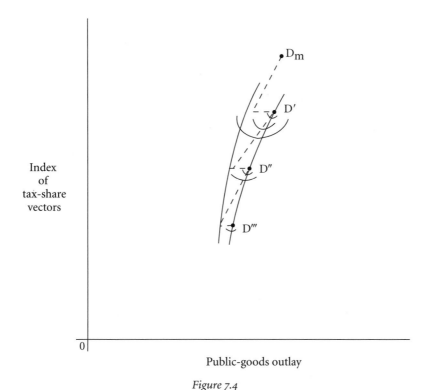

Public-goods outlay

Figure 7.4

is made from *c* to *d,* Median's share *increases* despite the decrease in his minimal share as we shift up the scale. By contrast, High's share *decreases,* despite the increase in his maximum share as we move up the same scale.

The whole analysis is combined in Figure 7.5. As drawn, there is a broad range of possible intersections between the public-goods lines of optima for High and Median. Positions in the shaded area will not insure agreement between these two persons. But a position in this intersection does suggest that agreement may be produced by appropriately organized, and possibly minimal, changes in the tax-sharing arrangements. These can be of a localized sort and Low's tax-share need not be modified. If Low's line of public-goods optima cuts through this broad intersection, general agreement among all three parties seems possible. Some approximation to a Wicksellian solution can be realized in such cases.

Note that there is not likely to be agreement on tax-sharing schemes, even

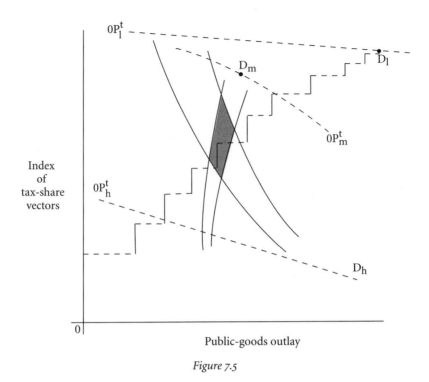

Figure 7.5

given a possible agreement on public-goods outlay. This conclusion resembles that reached in the earlier and simpler models. Also, if the two decisions, one on public-goods outlay and the other on the tax-sharing arrangement, should be taken separately and if majority rule prevails, the result may tend to be in the vicinity of D_m, also suggested by the earlier models.

This model should not be treated with great respect for its helpfulness, but neither should its suggestiveness be wholly neglected. The complexities that arise in the analysis of agreement should not obscure the underlying need to analyze the agreement processes. The problem to be analyzed is surely present under some circumstances. Agreement must be reached on both of the variables and many more besides, and these surely contain "publicness" elements in that all members of the community must adjust to the result.

As additional persons are added to the model, the ordering becomes more difficult, although the lexicographic method can formally be used for any number. Geometrical representation becomes messy, but the essentials of the analysis are not changed. As additional public goods, rules or institutions are taken into account, the prospects for agreement tend to increase in the relative sense discussed in Chapter 6.

Perhaps the test of usefulness for the models of this chapter is the question: Are hypotheses implied that can be tested by observations? Conceptually, tests can be made to determine to what extent the real-world solutions meet Wicksellian criteria. If, given the budgetary level and the tax-sharing scheme in existence, there is observed to be widespread disagreement concerning budgetary size and if this disagreement tends to be inversely related to level of income, this would provide strong evidence that a solution approximated by D_m is present. On the other hand, if the disagreement over budgetary size should be unrelated to income level, and if this disagreement should, in some relative sense, be minor, strong evidence is provided that some approximation to the Wicksellian results is achieved. Such evidence could never be conclusive, of course, because of the many alternative explanatory models that could be developed. It is worth recalling at this point that J. K. Galbraith, in his famous argument over the poverty of the public sector, implicitly assumed that the sustained budgetary position was of the sort depicted at D_m on the figures. The tax-sharing arrangement in being was held to prevent majority approval for the expanded spending programs that he considered to be desirable. His remedy was fully consistent with the analysis of this chapter. He proposed a substantial downward shift in the scale of tax-sharing in order to achieve the required approval for larger spending programs.

Private Decisions and Public Goods

This chapter draws attention to an important element of individual participation in collective choice that tends to be neglected in the theory of public goods in the standard sense. This neglect is evidenced in earlier chapters of this book as well as in the works of other scholars. Individual demand for a public good is derived from a utility function that does not include arguments for the cost-shares or tax-shares to be paid by other members of the community. Conceptually, an individual marginal evaluation schedule (or demand schedule under the appropriately restricted assumptions) is related to tax-prices or tax-price offers. This schedule allows us to talk about the behavior of the individual in "voting for" or "voting against" particular spending proposals. In this analysis, it is acknowledged that individuals cannot privately select preferred outcomes and that these must be determined by some group decision rule. But the analysis does purport to explain individual participation in this process, and, in this elementary explanation, individual demands are related only to tax-prices or tax-price offers in the direct and explicit sense.

The neglected element is the "publicness" of the tax-share choice. The individual chooses public-goods quantities, not only in relation to the total and marginal tax-prices that he expects to be confronted with, but also in some relation to the whole tax-sharing scheme or arrangement which allocates tax-shares between himself and other members of the group. Introspective experiment can make the importance of this element clear. Consider your own possible participation in, say, a community referendum on a proposed public outlay for improvement in municipal park facilities. Suppose that your own share in the tax-cost is equivalent under two separate financing alternatives. Suppose, however, that one of these alternatives exempts all high-income persons from taxation while the other scheme exempts all low-income persons. It seems evident that you will have some definite preferences as between the two tax-sharing schemes, a preference which you are required to express if these alternatives are themselves presented for group choice.

The publicness of tax-sharing arrangements requires that the individual pay some attention to the whole structure of payments. Recognition of the possible influence of this element on his behavior should not, however, blind us to the primary significance of his own tax-share in determining his behavior pattern. The theory of public goods remains incomplete when this element is wholly neglected, but such neglect is justified in the preliminary stages of inquiry when the purpose is that of isolating the most important influence on the demand for public goods.

In choosing both a quantity of public goods and a tax-sharing scheme for financing this quantity, the individual participates in a collective decision process that he recognizes as such. He is choosing *for others* as well as for himself. This very setting will tend to make him consider the relative positions of others. This situation may be compared with that faced by the individual in competitive market organization. In the latter, he does not explicitly recognize the indirect effect that his behavior will exert on others in the community. He tends to behave as if his actions exert no such influence. There is no explicit publicness in his choice calculus. The distinction between individual positions in these two situations provides the basis for some of the traditional socialist criticism of market order. The argument here, in summary, is that individuals, if forced to choose *for the group,* will surely widen their range of consideration. An acknowledgement of *some* difference in probable motivation for behavior in the two cases is not the same thing, however, as an acknowledgement of *categorical* difference. If, in fact, individuals could be predicted to choose among "public" alternatives on the basis of their own versions of group rather than an individual interest, we could discard much of the theory of public goods and of welfare economics, and devote time exclusively to analyses of the sort contained in Chapters 7 and 8. Conflicts would arise to the extent that personal definitions of group interest differ, and utility functions of the standard variety simply would not exist.

Bibliographical Appendix

The geometrical constructions of Chapter 7 are derived, generally, from the works cited previously in connection with Chapter 6, primarily those of Duncan Black. For the particular applications to the simultaneous choice of public-goods outlay and tax-sharing schemes, the constructions for the two-person model closely parallel those presented by Leif Johansen ["Some Notes on the Lindahl Theory of Determination of Public Expenditures," *International Economic Review,* IV (September 1963), 346–58]. Figure 7.1, in the text, is substantially equivalent to Johansen's Figure 3. Although Johansen does not extend his formal analysis beyond the two-person (two-group) model, some of his critical comments on the Lindahl model, generally, are also relevant to the discussion of this chapter. In his book [*Public Economics* (Chicago: Rand McNally, 1965)], notably Chapter 6, Johansen's geometrical construction is less detailed, although other comments are expanded beyond those in his paper.

Johansen's point of departure is Erik Lindahl's classic work [*Die Gerechtigkeit der Besteuerung* (Lund, 1919), relevant portions of which are translated as: "Just Taxation—A Positive Solution," and published in *Classics in the Theory of Public Finance,* edited by R. A. Musgrave and A. T. Peacock (London: Macmillan, 1958), pp. 168–76]. Lindahl's later papers are also relevant

["Some Controversial Questions in the Theory of Taxation," as translated into English from the German and also published in *Classics in the Theory of Public Finance;* also see, "Tax Principles and Tax Policy," *International Economic Papers,* No. 10 (London: Macmillan, 1959), pp. 7–23]. R. A. Musgrave summarizes the basic Lindahl contribution in his treatise [*The Theory of Public Finance* (New York: McGraw-Hill, 1959), pp. 74–78]. In an earlier paper, Musgrave discussed the Lindahl theory in some detail ["The Voluntary Exchange Theory of Public Economy," *Quarterly Journal of Economics,* LIII (February 1938), 213–37]. A more recent and more exhaustive discussion of Lindahl's contribution, along with consideration of possible criticisms, has been published by J. G. Head ["Lindahl's Theory of the Budget," *Finanzarchiv,* Band 23, Heft 4 (October 1964), 422–54].

As several critics have noted, Lindahl's theory suffers in its extension to the political decision process. It is in this respect that Wicksell's seminal contribution seems superior. Wicksell was concerned with potentially applicable rules for making political choices on both public-goods outlay and on tax-sharing arrangements, and he did not develop his theory in an explicit two-person bargaining context.

Howard Bowen, in his early contribution to the modern theory, set the whole problem in a political context ["Voting and the Allocation of Resources," *Quarterly Journal of Economics,* LVIII (November 1943), 27–48, substantially reprinted in *Toward Social Economy* (New York: Rinehart, 1948), pp. 172–98]. In his treatise, Musgrave devotes a chapter to "Budget Determination Through Voting" [*The Theory of Public Finance,* Ch. 6]. Some parts of Musgrave's discussion are directly relevant to the material covered in Chapter 7.

The most complete treatment of tax systems, considered as "public," is contained in the work of Charles J. Goetz [*Tax Preferences in a Collective Decision-Making Context* (Ph.D. dissertation, University of Virginia, 1965, available through University Microfilms, Ann Arbor, Michigan)]. Goetz examines group agreement on tax systems largely independent of group agreement on public-goods outlay, except as the recognition of underlying interdependence affects individual preference patterns. One portion of Goetz's argument was published earlier ["A Variable-Tax Model of Intersectoral Allocation," *Public Finance,* XIX (No. 1, 1964), 29–41].

The possible differences between individual behavior in the choice of private goods and in the choice of public "goods" was stressed by William J. Baumol [*Welfare Economics and the Theory of the State* (Cambridge: Harvard University Press, 1952; Second revised edition, 1965)]. In an early paper of my own, I attempted to examine these differences in some detail ["Individual Choice in Voting and the Market," *Journal of Political Economy,* LXII (August 1954), 334–43, reprinted in *Fiscal Theory and Political Economy* (Chapel Hill: University of North Carolina Press, 1960), pp. 90–104]. The indirectness of the effects of individual behavior in the market process and its effect is discussed in the book by Robert A. Dahl and C. E. Lindblom [*Politics, Economics, and Welfare* (New York: Harper, 1953)]. In a relatively recent paper, I have discussed some of the consequences for modern welfare economics arising out of the presumed categorical differences in individual behavior in voting and market processes ["Politics, Policy, and the Pigovian Margins," *Economica,* XXIX (February 1962), 17–28].

Recent works, in preliminary form, by Robert Dorfman and by Martin Shubik examine aspects of public-goods theory in a collective-choice setting [Dorfman, "General Equilibrium with Public Goods," Working Paper No. 95, Institute of Business and Economic Research, University of California at Berkeley, June 1966; Shubik, "Notes on the Taxonomy of Problems Concerning Public Goods," AD 633 546, Defense Documentation Center, April 1966]. Albert Breton has attempted to relate the theory of public goods to the theory of collective decision-making ["A Theory of the Demand for Public Goods," *Canadian Journal of Economics and Political Science,* XXXII (January 1966), 455–67].

8. The Institutions of Fiscal Choice

Introduction

The analytical models introduced in earlier chapters of this book are skeletons, as all useful analytical models must be. They are designed to isolate important relationships in any theory of the demand and supply of public goods. Such a theory must be supplemented with the data of experience before any genuine understanding of fiscal process can be achieved. This filling in, this discussion of the historical-institutional record, is a task for scholars whose competence differs from my own. Although this book is limited to the models of analysis, one aspect of the theory itself remains to be discussed. In keeping with the metaphor above, the ossification of the skeletons must be examined. Are there logical derivations or analytical reasons for the built-in rigidities in the institutions of fiscal choice? The theory of the demand and supply of public goods must be supplemented by a *theory of fiscal institutions* before our task is finished. Public goods are demanded and supplied through processes that are themselves selected at some stage and apparently for reason. We need to understand something of the logic of institutional choice even if we cannot discuss this in great detail.

The distinction between the theory of institutions, to be examined, and the theory of demand and supply, previously examined, is one that may not seem automatically relevant to economists. Familiar analogies drawn from everyday experience in private life may prove helpful, although, as with all analogies, they will also be misleading in parts. Consider a man whose apartment is located one block from a corner newsstand. His early morning time schedule is such that on some mornings, unpredictable as to dates, he has adequate time to read the morning newspaper with his breakfast. On other mornings he must rush to work without time for even so much as a headline glance. He may, on mornings when his time is not so scarce, walk down to the newsstand and purchase the paper. Or, alternatively, he may choose to have a paper delivered to his apartment every morning, even though he recognizes that on many mornings this paper will go unread. The standard theory of the demand for morning newspapers helps us to understand the behavior of this man generally as he decides whether or not to purchase newspapers. This theory needs to be supplemented, however, by a "theory of institutions" in order to help us understand his behavior in deliberately *institutionalizing* his choice, even though he recognizes that, in specific instances, the results will be inefficient.

This initial overly simplified analogy may be replaced by a still-familiar but more complex one. Consider a community decision to install a set of traffic signals. It is surely obvious to the decision makers that on many occasions, when traffic flows are light, unnecessary delays to motorists will result. Presumably, the installation is made because these inefficiencies are predicted to be more than balanced by efficiency gains when traffic flows are heavy. The working of the institution over a whole sequence of situations must be considered, and, even here, the uniform application of an institution must be justified on cost-reducing grounds. If traffic regulation is relatively costless, the efficient scheme is to have a *different* institution during each period of traffic flow. A traffic patrolman can be stationed at the intersection during certain hours of the day. The fact that signals are installed which apply to all periods must suggest that, over the whole range of situations, this is a more efficient means of regulating traffic than the available alternatives. *Institutional choice* must be made on the basis of some comparison of costs and benefits over the whole sequence of expected events or periods.

The Recurrence of Choice

As the analogies suggest, the possible need to create institutions that will "make choices in advance" arises only when it is predicted that similar choice situations will be confronted recurrently, either over a sequence of time periods or over separated events. There is no need for our city dweller to make an "institutional" decision about the delivery of the *New York Times* if he is on a one-night stopover at a Manhattan hotel. The theory of choice in economics is concerned, for the most part, with such one-time or one-event decisions. At the least, the theory proceeds "as if" individuals choose anew among each set of alternatives that they face. The theory of public goods, as sketched out in earlier chapters, has been presented in this same manner. The choice among differing quantities of a public good (or among different bundles of public goods) and, also, the choice of tax-sharing arrangements has been discussed as if individuals participate in unique, one-at-a-time budgetary decision processes. The models contain no recognition, explicit or implicit, of the predicted repetition or recurrence of fiscal choices, roughly similar one to the other, over a whole series of time periods. In the early models, Tizio and Caio were simply assumed to face, each day, a new and current decision on the quantity of the public good and the manner in which they should share its cost. These early models of exchange, as well as the later ones of group decision processes, were limited in purpose to an explanation of the important elements determining outcomes of such unique choice events.

The Costs of Group Decision-Making

If the costs of making decisions are negligible, the analysis that concentrates on uniquely timed choices requires little or no emendation, even in the face of recurrent choice situations. Implicit in orthodox economic theory is the assumption that, for choices with which it is concerned, these costs are small enough to be ignored. This assumption can be defended because the theory here explains the behavior of individuals in privately organized market exchanges. These involve bilateral agreement between only two persons, and, even here, the presence of available alternatives on each side of the market converts effective choice-making into unilateral behavior. Consider the simple problem confronting the man who must decide whether to purchase corn flakes or porridge each morning in the cafeteria line. Presumably, he can make this choice in an instant and little effort or resource investment is required. He glances quickly at the relative prices, the attractiveness of the two items displayed, examines his own tastes and selects one or the other of the cereals. Once he has made this choice, the result is, for him, fully predictable. He gets what he wants; he is not required to reconsider his selection and change his mind for any reason. Economic theory, correctly, tries to explain the elements that go behind and inform such choices and simply ignores the minimal cost that the individual suffers in making up his mind even in this trivial choice process.

The individual will seldom, if ever, find it advantageous to routinize or institutionalize his morning's cereal selection even if he knows that he will be faced with this same choice each morning for a year. In fact, we should perhaps judge him to be eccentric if he is observed to refer to a "rule" which, let us say, makes his cereal selection depend on the throw of a die each morning. The same conclusion would be valid, although to a somewhat lesser degree, for more important market decisions made by individuals.

The categorical distinction to be emphasized here is that which arises between the level of individual or private choice in the market and group or collective choice with respect to the relative significance of decision-making costs. In this second situation, these costs become sufficiently important to warrant explicit analysis, analysis supplementary to that which explains one-period, nonsequential choice. In collective choice, the theory remains seriously incomplete unless this supplement is added. The element present here and absent from private choice is the *necessity for separate individuals to reach agreement.* As in choice of any sort, the individual must make up his own mind, and this in itself involves some cost. This need not be of concern, however, if this is all there is to it. In group decision, separate parties must, somehow, come to agreement on a single result, regardless of their own initial preferences. The absence of divisibility in the result does not allow them to turn to alternatives. An important cost factor is necessarily introduced that is relatively insignificant in private market choices. If the group interaction is small, negotiation and bargaining will take place. By the nature of the situation they face, individuals will invest resources in strategic bargaining, and this investment will be individually rational. They will try to secure group outcomes favorable to their own interests. Once the group becomes critically large, the costs of voluntary agreement may become prohibitive, so much so that individuals will forego the effort.

In either small or large groups, it seems obvious that the recognition of the importance of decision-making costs, along with the expectation that similar choice situations will recur over time, may suggest the relative efficiency of institutions or rules of choice. These may dramatically reduce the costs of making group decisions, although they do so necessarily at the cost of some in-period efficiency. Such institutions or rules must ossify the structure of in-period choice and must make particular outcomes less rather than more flexible. Over a whole series of choices, however, such institutions or rules may be more efficient than the relevant alternatives.

The Rules for Reaching Group Decisions

In a large-number political setting, the only one relevant for considerations of public-goods demand and supply, the first set of institutions or rules to be examined are those that define the manner of arriving at group or collective outcomes. These institutions and/or rules, as a set, make up the *political constitution*. The approach suggested here allows us to examine existing and potentially alternative constitutional rules in terms of efficiency criteria that are similar to those used in orthodox economic analysis. This institutional choice approach makes it conceptually possible to derive an explanation for a political constitution from the choices of individuals as they participate in the basic decision process on the rules that determine the procedures of group choice itself.

Something of this nature is required if we are to go beyond and behind the Wicksellian proposals for effective unanimity rules in the making of fiscal decisions. These proposals have been discussed several times in this book, and they are directly relevant to an understanding of the whole theory of public goods. A Wicksellian rule of unanimity is the political or institutional counterpart to the theory of choice that was developed in earlier chapters. Translated into political-choice terms, Pareto optimality becomes Wicksellian unanimity. The direct relationship between these two concepts is self-evident. Unless all members of the group agree to make a proposed change, some member or members must expect to be made worse off by the change; the proposal is disqualified by the Pareto-optimality criterion. Applied to positions, and not to proposals (a necessary distinction), if there is no change upon which unanimous agreement can be attained, then the initial or *status quo* position qualifies as Pareto-optimal. Wicksell and Pareto were roughly contemporaries and worked independently one from the other. Pareto's genius in developing the welfare criteria has been properly recognized. Wicksell's genius in relating political rules to orthodox efficiency notions in economics has not yet received its due.

Wicksell's contribution provides an indispensable groundwork for any further examination of political institutions or rules. It is necessary, however, to go beyond these simple efficiency limits, since even casual observation reveals that seldom, if ever, are unanimity rules (or even rules for relative unanimity) written into actual political constitutions. Experience surely suggests that efficiency in making group or collective decisions may necessarily involve departures from the restrictive Wicksellian limits, which would require that each single group choice be Pareto-Wicksell efficient. This conclusion applies to political choices in general, and not only to fiscal choices, although the latter are the primary subject of analysis here. This book is not the place, however, to discuss the derivation of a "theory of political constitutions" in general terms. This attempt has been made in other works, and repetition is not required save in capsule form. The essential point to be made is that nonunanimity rules for reaching group choices can be justified on efficiency grounds under the appropriate conditions.

Political constitutions embody a complex set of rules and institutions, and the analyst who does not construct abstract models will soon be lost in a maze of descriptive variety. One such abstract model is the simple-majority voting rule. This model is important in itself, and doubly so because it is widely held to be the central and characteristic feature of democracy. Considerable insight should be gained, therefore, into the formal properties of democratic structures when simplified models of direct majority voting are examined. This is the context within which the simple model for majority voting was introduced in Chapters 6 and 7. The model may be used here as merely illustrative of a whole set of "institutions of choice" that might be incorporated in a comprehensive evaluation of a political constitution.

Consider a community faced with a predicted series of decisions, both on the quantity and mix of public goods and on the means of sharing the costs among its citizens. The voluntary negotiation of agreed-on outcomes in each subperiod may be, and probably will be, prohibitively costly. The community adopts, explicitly or implicitly, simple-majority voting as the rule for reaching definitive results, and members agree to abide by the outcomes dictated by this rule. As it works itself out over time, there is perhaps some general expectation that, for the average or representative citizen, this decision rule is relatively more efficient than its alternatives. At least this should be the basis for its selection over alternative rules. Over time, any individual in the community will expect this rule to produce unfavorable results in particular instances, results that run counter to his own preferences. Public-goods projects which he urgently desires may not be undertaken because a majority of his fellow citizens does not agree with his evaluation. Or, conversely, he may be required to contribute to the costs of projects that he considers to be worthless. The efficiency justification for this rule, or for any other, must be found in the prediction that, on balance, the gains offset these in-period inefficiencies.

This is only a thumbnail sketch of the economic theory of majority rule. It is perhaps sufficient to suggest that any rule for making political choices must be evaluated on its own merits and against its relevant alternatives. If the decisions are largely technical ones, or if the case is one where any rule is better than no rule and differences among rules are insignificant (e.g., traffic control), delegation to bureaucratic decision makers may prove more efficient than simple-majority voting. If the decisions are predicted to be of major importance, effectively qualified majorities may be considered to be relatively efficient. For some issues and in some circumstances, one decision rule can be supported on efficiency grounds, for other issues and other circumstances another rule more closely meets efficiency criteria. It is incumbent on the analyst to examine each case and to isolate the important elements. Only in this way can a theory of institutional choice, at the level of political rules, be constructed.

Specific Fiscal Institutions

The discussion of political institutions and rules provides an essential preliminary to a discussion of the specific institutions of fiscal choice. The rules for reaching group decisions, briefly examined in the preceding section, are not likely to be applied uniquely to fiscal choices, as Wicksell seemed to hope might be the case. If simple-majority voting rules within legislative assemblies are the dominant means of making decisions about Blue Laws and Daylight Saving Time, the same rules are also likely to be adopted for making choices about the mix and quantity of public goods and about the means of allocating their costs. Even if efficiency considerations should dictate a different set of rules for fiscal decisions, and even if these considerations should be reflected in constitutional processes, it will still be useful to examine fiscal institutions separately from the rules governing the making of political decisions, including those on fiscal matters.

Given any set of political-decision rules, there may be *fiscal rules or institutions* which restrict the range within which collective results may emerge. This is yet another aspect of institutional choice, and this is the subject for examination.

Consider a community that has an established political constitution. This constitution requires the election of representative assemblies, and within these assemblies, decisions on budgetary matters are made by simple-majority voting. The constitution also requires that public-spending programs be approved each year. Faced with this situation, is there a need for supplementary rules to serve, in effect, as a "fiscal constitution"?

There may be two reasons why such rules are desirable. The first has already been discussed in connection with majority rule as a cost-reducing device, costs here being those of decision-making itself. Supplementary fiscal rules that serve to limit the range of majority-rule outcomes may effectively reduce the costs of decision. The second reason is quite different. Majority rule in political decisions may substantially reduce the costs of decision-making below those that would be present under the operation of a unanimity rule, but majority rule will necessarily increase the costs measured by in-period inefficiencies. Supplementary fiscal rules and institutions may well be desired to restrict the operation of majority rule, to restore to an extent the efficiency-generating characteristics of a near-unanimity rule without incurring the additional decision-making costs that resort to more restrictive political-decision rules would introduce. This suggests that political-decision rules and fiscal rules may be substitutes for each other, a relationship that will be discussed in some detail in the next section.

In earlier chapters, it has been implicitly assumed that the collective decisions on *both* sides of the budget are worked out in detail in each budgetary period, based on some relationship between the demand for public goods and the costs of supplying them. The most elementary criteria for rational choice, at the collective as well as at the private level, suggest that costs are balanced off against benefits, and that this is facilitated by the retention of maximum flexibility in adjustment on both sides. It seems proper to infer from this that simultaneous consideration of the two public-decision variables, both the tax and the expenditure mix, is a fundamental requirement for efficiency. Observation of real-world fiscal structures suggests that this procedure is rarely, if ever, followed. Naively interpreted, the observed institutional rigidities can only produce undesirable results. Inflexibility in tax-sharing arrangements may prevent majority support of presumably desirable spending projects, and, conversely, the same inflexibility promotes majority support of some projects that are intrinsically inefficient. Economists who compute cost-benefit ratios are perhaps shocked at the results of inflexible political processes, which seems to reflect so little heed given to economists' advice.

A more comprehensive and critical approach suggests that the institutional structure may contain elements that make for efficiency but which are neglected in elementary choice theory. If the community predicts that fiscal decisions will be made each year, and that these decisions will be similar in many respects, individuals may agree to impose upon themselves, upon their legislative assemblies, rules that effectively define a fiscal constitution. Specifically, the community may preselect a set of tax-sharing arrangements, a tax system or structure, independent of the particular in-period choices to be made on the public-goods outlay. Considered exclusively from the one-period vantage point, this deliberate freezing of certain potential variables implies inefficiencies in results. The range of in-period choice is narrowed. Things may appear quite different, however, when a whole sequence of time periods is taken as the horizon for judgment. If there are no rules for tax-sharing that are to be followed, if no standing rules for the allocation of the costs of public goods are carried forward from one year to the other, the whole cost-distribution issue comes up for grabs each time. The community must face anew the tedious and resource-using task of hammering out acceptable terms of cost-sharing, which, even with only a simple legislative majority required for decision, may prove formidable indeed. In addition, if no such rules for tax-sharing are imposed constitutionally, the possible exploitation of dissident minorities that may be accomplished fiscally by majority coalitions is substantially larger than in the presence of such rules. Potential exploitation costs as well as decision-making costs may be reduced by specific tax-sharing rules that take on constitutional characteristics.

Any set of rules will limit the range of outcomes that can emerge from the political process, given any rule for making group choices. If all public goods to be financed are selected under the constraint that all revenues must be raised, say, by a proportional tax on incomes, some possible outcomes will not be feasible. The advantages and disadvantages of imposing such rules must, of course, be examined case by case and judgment cannot be dispensed with. But it seems possible to suggest influences on community attitudes toward a fiscal constitution. Under what conditions will it seem relatively efficient to lay down tax-sharing rules constitutionally? By "constitutional" in all this discussion, I mean only to refer to rules and institutions that continue in being from period to period, independently of choices made within periods. I am not concerned with semantics.

One primary consideration must be the nature of the goods and services that the community is expected to supply collectively. As a preliminary to more detailed analysis, the hypothesis suggested is that general rules on tax-sharing are more acceptable when the goods and services to be publicly supplied provide general benefits rather than special benefits. This begs several questions concerning definitions, questions that have already been discussed in some detail earlier. Ignoring real-world relevance for the moment, assume initially that the community is expected to supply publicly only goods and services that yield equal flows of homogeneous-quality consumption services to each citizen. In this extreme model, individual demands for public goods and services will differ, but they will do so only because (1) income-wealth positions differ, and (2) utility functions differ. To ignore for the moment income-generated differences in demand, assume that all members of the community earn equal incomes and have the same wealth.

Under what circumstances will members of this community find it relatively efficient to impose a constitutional rule to the effect that all collective goods are to be financed by equal-per-head taxes? If an individual predicts that, over a whole series of separate decisions on budgets, his own demands will be more or less randomly distributed relative to those of his fellow citizens, he may consider that resort to such a constitutional rule is an efficient means of reducing decision-making costs, while at the same time reducing the likelihood that he will suffer undue discrimination at the hands of majority coalitions. On the average, over the whole set of choice situations, this rule will not generate outcomes grossly unfavorable to him, and he is saved the bother of worrying about changed tax-sharing arrangements for each public good in each period. By contrast, suppose that an individual expects that, generally, his own demands for public goods over all goods and over the whole sequence of periods is likely to be well above or well below those of most of his fellow citizens. Here he may not agree to an equal-sharing rule laid down in advance, since he would prefer some alternative rule or even separately negotiated sharing arrangements in each choice situation.

Individuals do not, of course, have equal incomes, and we can relax this assumption while remaining within the extreme model where it is expected that only pure public goods and services will be supplied publicly. The possibility of securing agreement on general fiscal rules will depend on the establishment of some relationship between the predicted demands for publicly supplied goods and external criteria that reflect economic position. If all goods and services are expected to exhibit positive income elasticities for all consumers, some agreement seems plausible on tax-sharing schemes that relate payments to income or wealth. Schemes with this characteristic will not be unduly discriminatory, provided that individuals expect their own tastes, relative to those of others, to range widely over the whole set of budgetary decisions.

The pure publicness model must, of course, be dropped, but it remains useful as a benchmark. Consider goods and services that yield general benefits, in the sense that service flows are provided to substantially the whole membership of the collectivity. These goods, of the fire-station type, yield different physical flows of services to different persons in the group. They will be valued differently, not only because of income and taste differentials, but also because of the basic differences in provision of services. Even here, however, an individual may accept certain tax-sharing rules as relatively efficient if he anticipates some randomization in the separate demands for separate goods in the budgetary mix and over time. To refer to the fire-station example, the individual who lives some distance from the facility may think that, when all other publicly supplied goods and services are taken into account along with fire protection, he will be "closer" to some, "farther" from others. He may get relatively little fire protection from the distant fire station, but, balanced off against this, he may have more children to be publicly educated than the man who lives next door to the firehouse. On this sort of logic, the individual may support a general tax-sharing scheme, say proportional income taxation, to finance all public goods over all periods.

As we have suggested on several occasions, governments supply goods and services that do not fit the publicness category in any sense. Suppose that an individual expects the collectivity to supply goods and services that are, for the most part, designed specifically to provide services to particular individuals or groups in the community. Under such conditions, an individual seems less likely to support *general* tax-sharing schemes at the constitutional-institutional level. He may anticipate that he will be on the receiving end of the bargains a representative share of the times, and therefore some fiscal rules may be desirable. He should also recognize, however, that, with special-benefit goods and services, constitutional rules requiring general taxation will produce a relative oversupply of public goods, given the operation of majority rule. In a regime where the publicly supplied goods and services are expected to be of the special-benefit type, tax-sharing rules laid down in advance should provide for special rather than general taxes.

Regardless of the logical or nonlogical origins that may have guided their evolution, we observe real-world fiscal systems characterized by "constitutional" rules on tax-sharing. Tax legislation is considered independent of budgetary or spending legislation, and structural changes in the tax system are discussed as quasi-permanent institutional reforms. The basic income tax law in the United States remained substantially unchanged from 1954 to 1964. Budgetary decisions on the amount and the mix of goods and services are made within a revenue system which acts as a "constitutional" constraint. One of the two public variables, the allocation of tax shares, is frozen by pre-selected rules. Decision-making on the remaining variable (or set of variables) on the spending side is facilitated even if the range of possible results is narrowed.

Substitution Between Political-Decision Rules and Fiscal Rules

Wicksell proposed more flexible tax-sharing arrangements as a means of securing the acceptance of spending programs by a substantially larger-than-majority proportion of the political community. These suggestions for greater flexibility in tax-sharing accompanied his proposals for applying the rule of unanimity, or of relative unanimity, to the making of collective choices on fiscal matters. Because of this inclusive rule for political choice, individuals and groups would be protected against possible majority exploitation. For this reason, they should then be willing to explore more flexible tax-sharing schemes. Until and unless something akin to the unanimity rule for making collective choices is established, however, institutional constraints imposed on tax-sharing become partial substitutes for the more inclusive political-decision rules. The degree of substitutability between these two sets of institutions was not fully appreciated by Wicksell.

The relationship may be demonstrated in a simple example. Assume that all individuals in the community share identical public-goods preferences; all utility functions are the same and all incomes are equal. Assume further that all goods to be supplied collectively are known to provide equal flows of consumption services to all persons. In this extreme model, a tax-sharing rule that dictates equal shares among persons becomes substantially equivalent to a political-decision rule of unanimity. If costs are to be shared equally by all citizens, and this is laid down as a constitutional rule, the outcomes with respect to public-goods quantities will be identical under *any and all* rules for making group choices. An individual should, in this case, be indifferent as to the particular manner in which group choices are made, and he should select among these strictly on some least-cost criterion. The delegation of decision-making authority to any single person will produce results identical to those that would be forthcoming under majority voting rules or even under a unanimity rule. The collective-choice rule does not matter here *because* the fiscal rule, given the conditions of this model, prevents any opportunity for differential or discriminatory treatment. If one person should be granted power of decision for the community, he cannot use this power to advance his own private interest *vis-à-vis* his fellows. He cannot, by the assumptions of the model, choose that the collectivity provide goods and services which are differentially beneficial to him. And he cannot, because of the equal cost-sharing rule, secure the benefits of publicly supplied, pure public goods and services without paying his own *pro rata* share of their costs.

Only in this rarified model will the selection among political-decision rules make no difference to the outcomes defined in terms of public-goods quantities. If the adherence to the equal-sharing rule is dropped, a potential dictator could escape costs by insuring that taxes be imposed only on others than himself. And a majority coalition could do likewise by imposing the bulk of the costs of all public goods on the minority. Protection against discriminatory treatment comparable to that provided by the equal-sharing rule would require a political-decision rule of effective unanimity.

Institutional constraints can also operate on the spending side of the budget. Even with an equal-sharing rule, if special-benefit projects are allowed, the political-decision rule makes a major difference in the expected outcomes. The limitation of public supply to those goods and services that do provide general benefits is in itself a major protection against undue discrimination on the spending side. And to the extent that this limitation is effective, not only are tax-sharing rules less urgently required, but less-inclusive political-decision rules can also be accepted.

In practical effect, the Wicksellian proposals amount to a substantial relaxation of both tax-sharing rules and budgetary criteria in exchange for a substantial tightening up in the rules for reaching political-collective decisions. In real-world settings, some compromise among these three sets of rules or institutions is likely. In Western democratic countries, political decisions are reached by majority voting in legislative assemblies, either unicameral or bicameral in nature, constrained by their own rules of procedure, and by varying interactions between legislative and executive authority. The range of fiscal outcomes that this process can produce is further limited by agreed-on rules that define, as it were, a "fiscal constitution." Severe limits are placed upon the powers to impose arbitrarily discriminatory taxes, and less restrictive but still meaningful constraints are placed on the type of goods that may be provided publicly.

Recognizing this is not the same as suggesting that existing or observed constitutional arrangements as to political-decision rules, tax-sharing rules and budgetary criteria are necessarily, or even probably, the most efficient set that can be found. Gross inefficiencies may exist, and to locate these should be one of the purposes of analysis. The discussion here is intended to suggest only that a structure of fiscal rules, which does limit the flexibility of adjusting either taxes or the mix of public goods, can be derived from basic efficiency considerations, given the absence of Wicksellian unanimity in making political decisions. If individuals could be assured that tax-spending programs would be enacted only upon the approval of substantially the whole community, resort to additional rules on either tax-sharing or on the range of public goods supplied would be inadvisable. In this case, such constraints could only make decisions more costly, and they could not provide additional protection against exploitation. If individuals should differ substantially in their demands for goods, agreement is facilitated to the extent that tax-sharing schemes can be adjusted and other, possibly special-benefit, goods also provided. However, majority voting rules, as qualified in actual structures, provide means of reaching collective decisions without explicit agreement among all persons and groups. In this political context, fiscal rules that serve to limit (sometimes severely) the alternatives available may tend to generate more efficient outcomes over the whole sequence of choice situations.

A Rehabilitation of Traditional Tax "Principles"?

An analysis of the "institutions of fiscal choice" suggests that, under appropriate conditions, members of a politically organized community may find it relatively efficient to adopt tax-sharing arrangements independently of particular choices on the quantity and mix of goods and services publicly supplied, arrangements or rules that are explicitly designed to be constitutional. They may be chosen with the intent that they shall remain in effect over a whole, and unpredictable, set of separate choice situations, and over a sequence of budgetary periods. In this context, it is evident that alternative tax-sharing proposals or plans must be examined in terms of some general criteria of efficiency, and not as related to specific benefit imputations from identifiable goods and services. In one respect at least, the approach seems to provide methodological legitimacy to the time-honored tradition in neoclassical public finance, the discussion of tax "principles" in rather complete isolation from any consideration of public expenditures. Does the institutional approach suggested come down, finally, to a rehabilitation of the traditional treatment after all?

The answer to this question can be affirmative only in a highly qualified sense. The end result is the same: Independent or separate principles are applied only to one-half of the fiscal account. In neoclassical public-finance theory, however, the framework for analysis is entirely different from that which suggests the institutional-choice approach. The neoclassical tradition contains no exceptions among English-language scholars, but this conclusion must be qualified, especially when Italian scholars are taken into consideration. Among the latter group, de Viti de Marco comes perhaps closer to the institutional-choice emphasis than any other scholar. In the strict English-language tradition, the independent derivation of tax-sharing norms has its origin in the "unproductive" consumption notions of the classical economists. Government outlay was considered "unproductive," and there was, by implicit assumption, no return of services to the citizens who were taxed. This neoclassical model of public finance was not wholly divorced from an underlying and assumed model of political organization, as Wicksell acutely noted. In a political regime that devotes the bulk of government outlay to the maintenance expenses of a single sovereign, or even of an elite, there is no demonstrable return flow of services to the taxpayers. This essentially non-democratic model of political order was, perhaps unwittingly, carried over into the democratic era by economists who paid little heed to their political presuppositions. In English-language neoclassical public finance, there was no indication that the governmental machinery is organized on democratic forms. No scholar called attention to the simple fact, noted in Italy first by Ferrara and then more emphatically by de Viti de Marco, that those who bear the costs of public services are also the beneficiaries in democratic structures. Somewhat surprisingly, English-language public finance continued to rest on the implicit assumption about taxes that Einaudi aptly labeled *imposta grandine*, literally translated as "hailstorm tax." Tax principles were discussed as if, once collected, revenues were removed forever from the economy; taxpayers, both individually and in the aggregate, were held to suffer real income losses.

Within such a framework, it followed more or less rationally that taxes should be analyzed in terms of their ability to satisfy certain minimization criteria. Taxes were discussed in terms of "least-aggregate sacrifice," the most sophisticated of the utilitarian principles, and in terms of least-price distortion, the somewhat more widely accepted norm for market efficiency. Principles of "just" taxation and of "efficient" taxation were not based in any way on the imputation of benefits from public goods and services.

By contrast and/or by comparison, the independent consideration of tax-sharing arrangements that emerges from the institutional approach is derivative from specific predictions about the pattern of benefit imputations over many goods and many periods. In this sense, the approach falls within "benefit principle" ideas, which were largely rejected in neoclassical theory. In its more narrow and more familiar interpretations, the benefit principle lays down norms for tax-sharing that relate individual payments directly to spending flows from particular goods and services in particular budgetary periods. The institutional approach allows this direct link between specific benefit imputations and tax-shares to be broken, but the justification for this step lies in the predictability of patterns of imputations over many goods and many periods. Given certain patterns of this sort, generalized criteria for efficient tax-sharing can be discussed independently of the allocation of public expenditures.

The setting is clearly different in the two models, despite the similarity in result, and, quite possibly, also in the specific norms for tax-sharing that may be derived. De Viti de Marco showed that either proportional or progressive income taxation could be justified on the basis of a model that is quite close to the institutional-choice approach, a model that contained explicit recognition of the productivity of publicly supplied goods and services. The institutional-choice approach provides a synthesis of sorts between the neoclassical ability-to-pay theory of taxation and the continental benefit theory of taxation. The neglect of the expenditure side in the former is eliminated, while, at the same time, the specific in-period connection between tax-shares and benefit-imputations in the latter is no longer necessary. In this synthesis, however, the derivation of tax-sharing norms is much more difficult than either the ability-to-pay or the benefit approach suggests. Criteria of efficiency and fairness reduce to the same thing, but in comparing alternative arrangements in terms of these many more variables must be taken into account than traditional discussion has implied. The increased importance of uncertainty pervades the whole analysis. While some of the established norms can be derived from this approach, other long-established principles can be shown to be demonstrably faulty.

Conclusion

The analysis of existing and alternative tax-sharing and expenditure arrangements or rules in a long-period constitutional setting will not be carried out here. The discussion of this chapter has been limited to pointing out the relevance of this institutional analysis to any comprehensive theory of demand and supply of public goods and services. The fact that an analysis of the institutions of fiscal choice must be appended to the more restricted pure theory of public-goods allocation does not, of course, make the latter analysis irrelevant or unnecessary. The pure theory, which has been the subject matter of earlier chapters, must be essentially completed before institutional analysis can even begin. Even with the pure theory of public goods, much remains to be done, and the theory of fiscal institutions has only been developed in bits and pieces. For this reason, I have not, in this chapter, tried to analyze tax-sharing and budgetary rules in terms of specifically defined alternatives. I have not, for example, tried to examine the possible derivation of a rule for proportional income taxation as opposed to one for progressive income taxation. One of the important and largely incomplete tasks of fiscal research and scholarship is precisely this of applying the institutional-choice methodology to the whole range of potentially important fiscal alternatives.

Bibliographical Appendix

Chapter 8 is the only one in the book which summarizes, in a modified context, material that I have, jointly or independently, developed in greater detail in other works. The derivation of a set of basic constraints governing the rules for making collective choice, a political constitution, from the efficiency calculus of individuals is the primary objective of a book that was written jointly with Gordon Tullock [*The Calculus of Consent* (Ann Arbor: University of Michigan Press, 1962, 1965)]. The extension of this approach to apply to the choice of fiscal institutions along with the effects of such institutions on individual behavior in politics is the objective of my later book [*Public Finance in Democratic Process* (Chapel Hill: University of North Carolina Press, 1967)].

The importance of analyzing the choice of rules, as distinct from choices made under constraints imposed by a set of existing rules, has been impressed on many scholars in separate fields in the last two decades. This has been one of the by-product contributions of game theory, a contribution that has perhaps been as significant as the more specific theory itself. The standard references may be cited [J. Von Neumann and O. Morgenstern, *The Theory of Games and Economic Behavior* (Princeton: Princeton University Press, 1944); R. D. Luce and H. Raiffa, *Games and Decisions* (New York: John Wiley and Sons, 1957)]. My own attention to this vital distinction owes much to many oral discussions with Rutledge Vining; his approach is perhaps best summarized in his review of economic research [*Economics in the United States of America* (Paris: UNESCO, 1956)].

An important, and closely related, development has been taking place in the discussion among philosophers over "rule-utilitarianism," most notably in the works of John Rawls ["Justice as Fairness," *Philosophical Review,* LXVII (April 1958), 164–94; "Constitutional Liberty and the Concept of Justice," *Nomos VI,* edited by C. Friedrich and J. Chapman (New York: Atherton Press, 1963); and, somewhat earlier, "Two Concepts of Rules," *Philosophical Review,* LXIV (January 1955), 3–32]. Rawls's approach has been recently applied to the income-distribution problem by W. G. Runciman [*Relative Deprivation and Social Justice* (London: Faber & Faber, 1966)].

There are, without doubt, similarities between the approach suggested and that taken by the American institutionalists, perhaps notably by J. R. Commons, although I am not specifically familiar with this body of scholarship. The influence of Frank H. Knight upon my own thinking should be acknowledged, and he is, in a broad sense, properly classified as an "institutionalist," especially in his less technical works [*The Ethics of Competition* (London: Allen and Unwin, 1935); *Freedom and Reform* (New York: Harper, 1947)].

As suggested in the text, the public-finance theorist who comes closest to having developed, although not explicitly, an approach consistent with an institutional-choice emphasis was Antonio de Viti de Marco [*First Principles of Public Finance,* translated by E. P. Marget (New York: Harcourt Brace, 1936)].

9. Which Goods
Should Be Public?[5]

The theory of public goods, as partially sketched out in early chapters of this book, is not a theory of public organization or supply, in either a normative or a positive sense, although it has been interpreted to be such by many scholars. In Samuelson's early and rigorous formulation, goods were classified into two polar categories, purely private and purely public. The allocative norms of modern welfare economics, which were developed in application to private goods, were then extended to public goods, as defined. Given the use that has often been made of these allocative norms with reference to private goods, it is understandable that organizational-institutional implications were read into the theory of public goods from the outset, regardless of the intent of the theory's original proponents. In a sense, and despite the apparent circularity, the implication that "public goods should be public" seemed a natural one. And, of course, linguistic philosophers would suggest that the very usage of the term "public" itself carried substantive overtones for organizational policy.

I have tried to demonstrate in earlier chapters that the formal models of this theory of allocation are considerably more general than the restriction

---

5. This chapter is not well integrated with the other parts of this book, and earlier attempts to locate the material elsewhere in the manuscript were not successful. Although the analysis builds on the models previously discussed, a new question is introduced which cannot be adequately explored in all of its complexities. Despite this acknowledged incompleteness, I have decided to include the chapter because of its relevance for the interpretations that many scholars, correctly or incorrectly, have placed on the modern theory of public goods, and finally, because of the fundamental and general interest of the question itself.

to polar cases might suggest. My emphasis has been placed, not on the manner in which goods are classified in some descriptive sense, but on the manner in which *goods are actually supplied.* This approach allows us to divorce entirely the allocative theory from the organizational implications. It does not, however, resolve the organizational-institutional question that remains of central importance. What goods and services should a community supply publicly through political-governmental processes rather than privately through market processes?

This is one of the vital questions in any theory of institutional choice, a theory introduced and discussed in Chapter 7 in general terms only. The allocative theory of public goods should surely be of some assistance in answering this question. It should provide a basis for an organizational-institutional theory, whether the latter be framed in normative or positive terms.

The Question Stated

What specific question must this theory ask, and try to answer? Despite the normative "should" in the chapter's title, I want, to the extent possible, to develop a theory that retains positive content. Under what circumstances will individuals as participating members of a politically organized community select collective organization as the means of supplying a particular good or service? The economists' stock response to this question is familiar: "When collective organization is more efficient than its alternatives." This answer says nothing and is tautological. Theory must go considerably beyond such limits if it is to be at all helpful in explanation and prediction.

The question rephrased becomes: Under what circumstances will collective-governmental supply be more efficient than private or noncollective supply? Here the standard response no longer holds, and the economist must answer on the basis of some comparative analysis of alternative institutions. The results that may be predicted to emerge from publicly organized supply must, in each case, be compared with those that may be predicted to emerge from noncollective, voluntarily organized, market supply.

Analysis here can commence with the calculus of an individual who is confronted with a choice as to the preferred organization of supply of a good or service at some conceptual stage of constitutional decision. This calculus reduces to a comparative evaluation of all institutional alternatives in terms of expected benefits and costs, both defined in present values, and both embodying major uncertainties. Alternatives must be compared on a quasi-permanent basis. No remotely relevant theory could be derived on the assumption that the organization of supply changes from one time period to the next.

The Divisibility Spectrum

If the question is one of determining the most desirable form of organization, some means of ranking or classifying goods and services independent of organization must be found. Since the form of organization itself affects the physical characteristics of many goods and services, the development of any such independent criterion will be difficult. We shall proceed here "as if" an independent array can be developed, although some qualifying notes will be made at appropriate points in the discussion.

Initially we may consider arraying all possible goods and services along some divisibility spectrum or scale. At one extreme we include all "purely private" goods and services, those that are perfectly divisible among separate persons (consumers). The total supply of such a good or service is represented by the summation of the supplies available to all persons. If X is the total quantity available to the group, and if $x_1, x_2, \ldots,$ are quantities available to individuals, then

$$X = x_1 + x_2 + \ldots, + x_n.$$

At the end of our scale, we include those goods and services that are "purely public," those that are perfectly indivisible as to benefits among the separate persons in the group. Here, if X is the total quantity available to the group, this same quantity is also available to each and every individual in the group

$$X = x_1 = x_2 = \ldots, = x_n.$$

All other goods and services are then arrayed between these two extremes in accordance with the relative importance of "divisible" and "indivisible" elements. For goods and services along the spectrum between the two extremes, no simple algebraic definition comparable to the familiar ones above is possible. As earlier discussion showed, the problem of defining units becomes important here. For current purposes, it is sufficient to think of all in-between goods as including both divisible and indivisible elements in varying ratios.

The Range of the Publicness Interaction

One major flaw in the scalar ranking of goods and services solely by the divisibility-indivisibility characteristic should be apparent. Goods and services will not hold the same rank in the scale as the size of the group changes. It is necessary to supplement the ranking by a second one that describes the range or limit over which the indivisibility characteristic, if it exists, holds. An example will clarify. It is probable that the benefits from mosquito spraying are almost wholly indivisible over the set of families living in one small suburb. It is equally clear that the benefits from mosquito spraying become fully divisible as among residents of suburbs in different outlying areas of the city. As in the case with the degree of divisibility, we may think of a whole scale or spectrum that defines the limits of the interaction. At the one extreme, again, we have the purely private, fully divisible good or service, where this interaction is defined as being limited to the single consuming unit, the person or the family. At the other extreme, we have the good or service that is fully indivisible as to benefits over a group that is, conceptually, of infinite membership.

A Summary Classification

The two independent characteristics, degree of indivisibility and extent or range of indivisibility, may be represented in a single box diagram, Figure 9.1. Along the abscissa we measure the size of the interacting group. Along the ordinate we measure the degree of indivisibility, from zero at the origin to perfect indivisibility at the top. It now becomes possible for us to place any good or service somewhere in the box as it embodies these two characteristics.

The theory of public goods, as it was initially developed, tended to force all goods into the two sets represented at the origin on the one hand and at $0'$ on the other. Purely private or fully divisible goods and services that may be classified as falling at or near the origin may be put in category (1) for

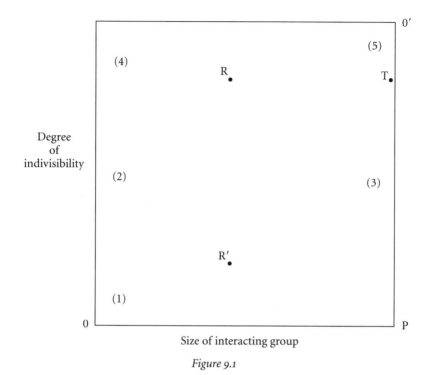

Figure 9.1

purposes of later analysis. Goods and services classified as falling at or near 0' may be put in category (5).

Three additional categories are noted in Figure 9.1, although no attempt is made to delineate precisely the areas of the figure to which these might refer. Category (2) includes those goods and services that are partially divisible, but which involve indivisibility or "publicness" elements only over a limited number of persons. Category (3) likewise includes goods and services that are only partially divisible. But here the publicness elements extend over a large number of persons. Category (4) covers those goods and services that are fully indivisible, or nearly so, but for which the range of indivisibility extends only over groups of limited size. Whole areas may be empty; few goods and services are likely to be found near the southeast corner of the diagram. It will be helpful to discuss the relevant categories falling between (1) and (5) in more detail.

(2) PARTIALLY DIVISIBLE GOODS AND SERVICES, WITH INTERACTIONS LIMITED TO GROUPS OF CRITICALLY SMALL SIZE

For a good or service that may be classified in this way, there must be some substitutability among consumption units, as among separate persons, but this is not one-for-one. If the total supply available to the group is fixed, the increase in consumption by one person will reduce the amount available to some other person, or persons, but not precisely by one unit, as in the purely private-good case, and not by zero, as in the purely public-good case. The "nonprivateness" extends, however, only over a relatively small number of persons. As the group size extends beyond these limits, all publicness elements vanish.

Examples of goods and services falling in this classification are those that involve *small-number externalities*. Fire extinguishers may be an illustration. A transfer of a fire extinguisher to my neighbor does not reduce my own fire protection from the extinguisher to zero, as would be the case with a purely private or divisible good or service. My neighbor's possession of the extinguisher continues to reduce somewhat the probability of fire damage to my property. However, this interaction is limited in range. The transfer of a fire extinguisher to someone who lives three miles from my house does reduce my own benefits from that extinguisher to zero, in which case the exchange becomes equivalent to that of a purely private good.

(3) PARTIALLY DIVISIBLE GOODS AND SERVICES, WITH INTERACTIONS EXTENDING OVER GROUPS OF CRITICALLY LARGE SIZE

This category includes the *large-number externalities,* or Pigovian externalities. There are both publicness and privateness elements in a good or service, but the publicness or indivisibility elements extend over a group that is critically large in size. An example is inoculation against communicable disease. The securing of a shot provides me with some privately divisible benefits but, also, it provides some benefits to all other potentially exposed persons in a large group. By comparison with the small-number interaction, in this instance many persons are effectively my neighbors. As we shall demonstrate later, the organizational-institutional differences between goods and services falling in (2) and (3) may be significant.

(4) Fully indivisible goods and services, but with interaction limited to groups of critically small size

This includes those goods and services that are characterized by the fact that there can be no increase or decrease in the quantity available for one person independently, so long as we are limited to groups of small size. Outside the common-sharing group, however, this pure publicness does not hold, and among separate small groups there may be no publicness elements at all.

Examples for this category are drawn from club-like arrangements, which provide the organizational norm for this set of goods and services. Swimming pools may be mentioned. The single pool may be equally available to all members of the swimming club, provided only that the size of the membership is limited.

Political-Group Size and the Structure of Property Rights

Before proceeding to use the classification scheme for purposes of trying to answer the organizational question posed in the chapter's title, two important additional qualifications must be introduced. Any actual classification of goods and services on the two-dimensional surface represented by Figure 9.1, along with the five numbered categories, must presume that the size of the overall political group is fixed exogenously and, also, that there is some existing structure of property rights.

The importance of the size of the political group can be shown easily. Suppose, initially, that the political group is of size P, that shown by the limits of interaction on Figure 9.1. Assume, now, that we classify a good as falling at point T, at or near the interaction limits. Suppose that the political unit is then incorporated into a larger jurisdiction of size 100 P. Clearly, the good falling at T no longer falls within category (5) or even nearly so. The extension in the size of the group has, in effect, shifted the classification from (5) to (4).

The relevance of some existing structure of property rights for any such classification scheme is also evident, but this is not so readily demonstrable. We may introduce an example. If the existing property laws do not allow land-owners to prosecute poachers, then all wooded areas are indivisible among many potential users. "Hunting land" would be classified as falling, say, at R, high on the indivisibility spectrum. On the other hand, if landowners can prosecute poachers, hunting land may be shifted to R', much lower on the divisibility scale.

For our purposes, we may specify simply that the size of the political group as well as the structure of property rights are fixed exogenously. This allows the two-dimensional classification of Figure 9.1 to be made without major inconsistencies or contradictions.

The Functions of Organization

Before we proceed to utilize this classification in answering the basic organizational question, it is helpful to recall the functions that any organization of supply must perform. Varying somewhat the familiar listing in Chapter 2 of almost every elementary economics textbook, these functions may be listed as follows:

1. determination of how much to produce—the allocation function
2. determination of how to cover the costs—the financing function
3. determination of how to distribute the benefits—the distribution function.

We shall, for simplicity, refer to these three functions as those of *allocation*, *financing* and *distribution*. The institutional-organizational structure selected, whether this be public, private or in-between, must perform all of these functions, jointly or separately.

A Pure Distribution Model

In order to simplify our analysis and to get somewhere with our two-dimensional classification, let us isolate only one of these three functions, that of distributing the benefits among persons. To do this, we resort to a highly unreal model that involves only the distributive function. Assume that goods and services falling anywhere on the classification matrix of Figure 9.1 are provided externally to the choosing group in fixed quantities. By this manna-from-heaven assumption, we rule out both the allocation and the financing problems.

What does the classification tell us about the problem of distributing supplies of goods and services among separate persons in the group?

Look first at goods and services classified in category (1). Unless the total amount supplied is sufficient to satiate the demands of all members of the group, there will arise some problem of distributing the scarce quantity among the separate users. If property rights are initially assigned to individuals in some fashion not related to their own evaluations, and if utility functions differ, efficiency criteria dictate that some transfers take place among separate persons. If a fully divisible numeraire good exists, trades among persons can be expected to emerge almost automatically. A pricing structure will arise out of the ordinary utility-maximizing behavior of individuals.

For goods and services that are roughly classified in category (2), there will exist some problem of distribution, both within the limits of the indivisibility interaction (which here is only partial) and among the separate small groups. A pricing-exchange system can be predicted to emerge to insure the resolution of the second of these problems in a manner equivalent to that for goods in (1). Within the limits of the small group itself, the partial indivisibility or publicness of the good or service requires that some bargained solution to the distribution problem be reached. Strategic behavior along with negotiating costs may prevent this in-group function being efficiently performed, but pressures toward efficiency will always be present. This case may be illustrated by the fire extinguisher. Suppose that the fixed quantity made available for distribution to the inclusive group, of size N, is $N/5$. How will this quantity come to be distributed both among and within small subgroups? Initially, we may presume that individuals will give consideration to the privately divisible elements inherent in the good. A market structure will emerge that will distribute the fire extinguishers to those consumers who place the highest evaluations on these, as privately divisible commodities. Such a distribution will not, however, take into account any of the spillover elements in benefits. All residents in some areas may possess fire extinguishers, and no residents in other areas. Faced with this prospect, we should expect cooperative small groups to form and to bid among themselves and among individuals for the scarce quantity. This will take place until some distribution is achieved that does take the benefit spillovers into account. Within the limits of each cooperating group, however, there remains a distribution problem. In whose residence shall the fire extinguisher be located? This must be the subject of negotiations within the group, and exchanges or compensations can be expected to resolve the issues. But significant negotiation costs are likely to arise.

Let us now examine goods and services that are classified in (4), leaving aside for the moment those in (3). For (4), the degree of indivisibility is great, but the range of the interaction is small. These goods are purely public but only for a small group of sharers. These are club-type goods and services, and we should expect sharing clubs to emerge as the appropriate organizational arrangements. Consider this in the context of our pure distribution model. Suppose that the quantity of a good made available to the all-inclusive political group is again $N/5$. Although a bit far-fetched here, let us remain consistent and use the swimming-pool example.

As with (2), we should expect prospective swimming clubs to be formed and to bid against each other, in units of a numeraire, until some distribution of the available pools is achieved. Within each sharing group, however, there will be *no* problem of distribution. This sharply distinguishes category (4) from (2). If, by classification, the goods fall in (4), there are no privately divisible elements present within the common sharing group, and, hence, the individual's utility cannot be affected by in-group distributional variations.

Remaining within the pure distribution model, we must now examine goods and services falling in category (3). Some problem of distributing any scarce quantity of a good will arise here because, by definition, there are privately divisible elements along with publicness elements. Given any fixed total quantity available to the inclusive group, along with some structure of property rights in this quantity, we should expect that an exchange system would emerge. Individuals would trade among themselves, in units of a numeraire, until the scarce quantity is distributed in accordance with the relative evaluations placed on the privately divisible elements.

As distinct from goods in category (2), however, no further voluntary behavior on the part of individuals could be expected to emerge. Somewhat paradoxically, the distribution in accordance with the relative evaluations placed on the privately divisible elements alone will be efficient, at least in the limiting model. Consider an example of inoculations for a communicable disease. The scarce supply comes to be distributed in accordance with the private-goods aspects alone; spillover benefits are wholly neglected. However, because the publicness elements extend over the whole of the large group, and because every person secures a spillover benefit equal to every other person no matter who gets an inoculation, no distributional change will modify the utility secured from the spillover benefits. This seemingly paradoxical conclusion holds only to the extent that a change in the distribution does not, in itself, modify the basic characteristics of the good itself.[6]

There remain only those goods and services that are found in category (5) in our two-dimensional classification. These are the polar public goods in which there are no privately divisible elements and for which the range of indivisibility is sufficiently large to include the whole of the membership of the political community. A useful statement can be made about such goods and services in this pure distribution model. The distribution problem wholly disappears. In fact, one means of defining a purely public good is to say that distribution costs are zero. Since, by definition and classification, the benefits are wholly indivisible among all members of the group, there will arise no problem of distributing the quantity that is available. The purely public good in this polar sense becomes equivalent to a "free good." This does not imply that individual demands for the good are satiated. Individual marginal evaluations may all be positive, but, so long as the benefits are wholly indivisible, no in-group pricing structure will emerge.

This approach emphasizes the inefficiency that must arise if any attempt is made to impose user prices on such a good or service. Since no problem of distributing scarce supplies among separate persons arises, any attempt at user pricing would be equivalent to converting such a good into one that falls

---

6. This is an important and necessary qualification. For goods and services exhibiting publicness over large groups (and inoculations may be excellent examples here) the *way* in which any available quantity is distributed may affect the degree and extent of spillover benefits generated. This is only one type of difficulty that is likely to be encountered in any attempt to classify goods and services by criteria that are inherent in the descriptive characteristics of the goods themselves.

within one of our other categories. However, this is only one of the sorts of inefficiencies that must be considered in any organizational comparison. We shall refer to this as *distributional* inefficiency.

Allocation and Financing

The pure-distribution or manna-from-heaven model has been discussed in some detail because it provides a helpful preliminary stage in using the two-dimensional classification scheme developed. It is only a preliminary stage, however, and the assumptions must be abandoned before serious organizational comparisons can be made.

Assume now that units of any good or service, falling anywhere in our classification, can be secured, from either domestic or foreign sources, at constant cost. (Our theory of public goods is sufficiently complex as it stands without introducing the additional problems that arise when decreasing or increasing costs on the production or supply side are present.) Assume further that this cost per unit is invariant over the separate organizational alternatives that are to be examined.

In this modified model, the organizational arrangement that is finally chosen for any good or service must perform the other two functions in addition to the limited distributional task isolated in the previous section. Some means must be found for determining how much of the good is to be provided; some *allocation* of resources to this good must be made. The securing of resources involves costs, and some means must be found for covering these; the *financing* function must be performed.

In the model which isolated the distribution function, it was shown that some market or pricing system would tend to emerge even in the performance of this limited task, at least for all goods save those in category (5). To the trained economist, orthodox micro-economic theory suggests that market or pricing structures can perform the other two functions simultaneously.

With goods and services that fall either in category (1), (2) or (4), collective or public activity in the strict sense may be limited to some establishment and enforcement of property rights, including contracts, and some policing of market structures against fraud and monopolistic combination. To an individual who tries to make the appropriate institutional-organizational comparison at some conceptual constitutional stage of decision, it seems un-likely that collective supply in the standard sense would be appealing for goods and services so classified. And if, for any reason, governmental organization is selected, efficiency criteria would dictate a structure that would closely par-allel the working of a market.

Serious consideration for explicit collectivization of supply seems likely to be limited to goods and services that are descriptively classified in categories (3) and (5). Goods and services in (3) contain both privately divisible and indivisible elements. An efficient organizational structure may embody some direct user pricing to facilitate the distributional task. To the extent that user pricing is employed, all three functions are simultaneously performed. Rev-enues are collected from consumers, and the total of these provides some in-dication as to the total quantity to be purchased by the community. How-ever, precisely because of the publicness or spillover effects simple efficiency criteria dictate that exclusive reliance on direct user pricing may be undesir-able. In a broad institutional setting, more complex efficiency criteria may still suggest exclusive reliance on direct user pricing. This would be the case when the commonality or publicness features are relatively insignificant. In such situations, organizational arrangements will not be different from those for goods in the categories (1), (2) and (4). These arrangements can be pre-dicted to emerge from the voluntary interactions of individuals in trading processes.

But when the commonality elements are considered to be significant, di-rect user pricing may be supplemented by tax-pricing. This combination nec-essarily implies that the organization of supply be collectivized, at least in the financing sense. The activity now lies within the domain of "public finance." Examples have already been mentioned, but these can be recalled here. In-oculations against communicable diseases may be provided at nominal fees to the individuals getting the shots, but the main share of the costs of financ-ing the program of immunization may be tax financed. Other examples may be public park facilities, garbage collection services, soil erosion for farmers, college education.

There remain the goods and services classified in category (5). These are purely public with the interaction extending all over members of the politi-cally organized community. In some in-group behavioral sense, these goods are "free." No problem arises in distributing any given supply among individual consumers, since, by definition, each consumer has available to him the full quantity provided. No allocation of shares is necessary.

Concentration on the divisibility characteristic and on the distributional problem alone might suggest that collective organization of supply is strongly implied for such goods and services. *A priori,* no such implication can be derived. No presumption can be established for either of the two broad institutional alternatives. The necessity that any organization perform the allocative and financing functions, along with the distributive one, removes any apparent presumption that collective organization is necessarily more efficient.

As we have previously shown, any attempt to charge prices for goods classified under (5) must involve *distributional inefficiency.* The marginal cost of allowing users access to the good is zero; efficiency criteria at this level dictate that the supply should be collectivized and "given away" to all potential users. But let us suppose that attention to these criteria of efficiency causes a good or service to be collectively organized. A decision is made to provide the good free to all users. Somehow the community must also determine how much to supply, and how to finance this quantity. If no user prices are to be charged, resort to the taxing mechanism is necessary. Any real-world taxing scheme must involve its own inefficiencies. The economist's benchmark of the lump-sum tax remains just that, an economist's benchmark. Any tax financing must produce the familiar *excess-burden inefficiencies.*

Additional inefficiencies are also likely to arise when the allocational decision is faced. If the supply is organized collectively, the allocation question must be settled, finally, by resort to some rule for making collective or group choices. Since separate individuals are likely to prefer different quantities of the good provided, under almost any taxing scheme, and since all persons must adjust to the same quantity, some persons are likely to be disappointed in each direction. For some individuals, the group choice will determine a level of public-goods provision that is below preferred levels. For other individuals, the level will be above preferred levels. These *allocational inefficiencies* must be considered along with the financing and distributional inefficiencies in any final organizational comparison.

If the provision or supply of a good is collectivized, the distributional efficiencies are reduced to zero in the case of the polar public good. But both financing and allocational inefficiencies emerge. If, on the other hand, arrangements are introduced which, in effect, convert the category (5) good into one that is privately divisible, distributional inefficiencies are necessarily introduced. Against this, however, the conversion of the good into one that allows for direct user pricing tends to reduce both the financing and allocational inefficiencies. To the extent that user financing replaces tax financing, the excess burden is reduced. And to the extent that revenues collected from users provide a criterion for determining the quantity of good provided, no explicit resort to a uniformly imposed and collectively chosen quantity is indicated.

The summary results of this analysis suggest that comparisons must be made on a case-by-case basis, even for goods and services that independently qualify as purely public in the category (5) sense. For such goods and services any attempt to introduce user prices will exclude some persons from access although the real costs of such access to the community do not exist. On the other hand, financing such goods through a tax structure and determining the quantity through a political-choice process introduce inefficiencies of other sorts. By necessity, comparisons are made in a world of second bests.

Public Supply and Public Production

In one sense, the title of this book may seem misleading despite the warning in the Preface. "The Demand and Supply of Public Goods" remains a discussion of demand with little reference to the organization of supply. This comment is relevant to this chapter where the basic elements of a theory of organizational choice are discussed. Here we have referred to public or collective organization of public-goods supply, but precisely what does this mean? Collectivization, or public organization, refers to the provision of the good, its financing and its distribution among separate demanders. Nothing in the discussion implies anything at all about the actual *organization of production*. Whether or not the good is purchased from privately organized firms and individuals in the domestic economy, purchased from privately or publicly organized supplying agencies abroad, or produced directly by government itself should depend on an efficiency calculus which compares these various alternatives. Collectivization of the supply, to meet individuals' private demands, says nothing about the relative efficiency of producing the good in any one of the several ways. This is a self-evident point, and it would not be necessary to mention here were it not for the widespread confusion that seems to exist.

The advantages of collectivization of supply, to be compared with the advantages of the institutional alternatives, stem from the possible indivisibility of a good or service *over separate persons as demanders*. This indivisibility, which arises in the consumption or utilization of a good or service, should not be confused with the more orthodox type of indivisibility that arises only in production, that which extends over *discrete units of production*. It is the second type of indivisibility that may exert some influence on the efficiency of organizational alternatives in producing the good. Once a decision is made to collectivize the supply of a good or service, the choice among alternative means of producing this supply is important, and careful analysis is required. This analysis, however, does not properly belong to the theory of public goods as we have interpreted it here.

Conclusion

This chapter has done little more than introduce some of the complexities of the question posed in its title: "Which Goods Should Be Public?" Any positive approach to this question must proceed on a case-by-case basis and provisional conclusions reached only after careful comparison of institutional alternatives in the broadest sense. The descriptive characteristics of a good or service, the technology of common-sharing and the range of such sharing, are important determinants of organizational efficiency. Care should be taken, however, not to presume that these characteristics, taken alone, allow *a priori* judgments to be made. The pound of *ceteris paribus* must be used with caution here, since other things are not at all likely to remain equal over the institutional variants that may be examined. The predicted working properties of the institutional structures, imposed as constraints on individual behavior, must be evaluated.

The modern theory of public goods, as it is widely interpreted, tends perhaps to overemphasize the descriptive characteristics of a good or service as a determinant of the efficient organizational arrangements to the neglect of other relevant factors. Analysis must start somewhere, however, and the modern theory can be extremely useful in providing the foundations upon which a more complete analysis can be built. Hopefully, some elements in such extended analysis have been suggested here, but this short book cannot include more than this.

Bibliographical Appendix

The recent exchange between Jora R. Minasian and Paul A. Samuelson is directly relevant to the question posed in Chapter 9 [Minasian, "Television Pricing and the Theory of Public Goods," *Journal of Law and Economics,* VII (October 1964), 71–80; Samuelson, "Public Goods and Subscription TV: Correction of the Record," *Journal of Law and Economics,* VII (October 1964), 81–84]. Otto A. Davis and Andrew Whinston have also provided a recent contribution ["On the Distinction Between Public and Private Goods," *American Economic Review Proceedings,* LVII (May 1967), 360–73]. The paper by R. N. McKean and Minasian also bears on some of the points ["On Achieving Pareto Optimality—Regardless of Cost," *Western Economic Journal,* V (December 1966), 14–23].

Other works that may be cited refer less directly to the central question and for the most part these analyze goods and services falling within particular sub-categories of the classification scheme presented. The recent work on small-number externalities by R. H. Coase deserves special mention ["The Problem of Social Cost," *Journal of Law and Economics,* III (October 1960), 1–44]. Other works in this same area of analysis include papers by James M. Buchanan and Wm. Craig Stubblebine ["Externality," *Economica,* XXIX (November 1962), 371–84]; by Ralph Turvey ["On Divergencies Between Social Cost and Private Cost," *Economica,* XXX (August 1963), 309–13]; by Davis and Whinston ["Externalities, Welfare, and the Theory of Games," *Journal of Political Economy,* LXX (June 1962), 241–62].

Large-number externalities, goods and services classified under (3) in Chapter 9, have been the subject of much practical interest in terms of air pollution and water pollution. Only a limited amount of this discussion is of theoretical interest, but especial note should be made of the works by Allen V. Kneese [*The Economics of Regional Water Quality Management* (Resources for the Future, 1964); "Quality Management of Water Supply," in *The Public Economy of Urban Communities,* edited by J. Margolis (Resources for the Future, 1965), pp. 170–91].

Three papers explore the predicted differences in results under different forms of organizing the provision of impure public goods [James M. Buchanan and Milton Z. Kafoglis, "A Note on Public Goods Supply," *American Economic Review*, LIII (June 1963), 403–14; James M. Buchanan and Gordon Tullock, "Public and Private Interaction Under Reciprocal Externality," in *The Public Economy of Urban Communities*, edited by J. Margolis (Resources for the Future, 1965), pp. 52–73; Wm. Craig Stubblebine, "Institutional Elements in the Financing of Education," *Education and the Southern Economy*, edited by J. W. Mackie, *Southern Economic Journal Supplement*, XXXII (July 1965), 15–34].

The problems raised by limited publicness in the spatial sense, where the range of common consumption does not extend over the entire area of the inclusive political jurisdiction, has been explicitly discussed by Albert Breton ["A Theory of Government Grants," *Canadian Journal of Economics and Political Science*, XXXI (May 1965), 175–87]. Some implications of this problem in a slightly different context are discussed in my paper ["An Economic Theory of Clubs," *Economica*, XXXII (February 1965), 1–14]. Some of the models developed by Mancur Olson are also relevant here [Mancur Olson, *The Logic of Collective Action* (Cambridge: Harvard University Press, 1965)]. In a somewhat more general setting, Mark Pauly has examined some of the organizational problems for goods in the (4) category with tools of modern game theory ["Clubs, Commonality, and the Core," *Economica*, XXXIV (August 1967), 314–24].

Some aspects of public-goods theory in application to local government finance are found in papers by Charles Tiebout and by Alan Williams [Tiebout, "The Pure Theory of Local Expenditure," *Journal of Political Economy*, LXIV (October 1956), 416–24; "An Economic Theory of Fiscal Decentralization," in *Public Finances: Needs, Sources, and Utilization* (National Bureau of Economic Research, 1961), pp. 79–96; Williams, "The Optimal Provision of Public Goods in a System of Local Government," *Journal of Political Economy*, LXXIV (February 1966), 18–33].

The degree of divisibility over units of production is relevant to the organization of production. Given full divisibility of this sort, production of a good may be competitively organized even if the supply is fully collectivized. By combining full divisibility in this respect with complete indivisibility among separate consumers, Earl Thompson has developed an extremely interesting variant of the standard public-goods theory. Under this combination of circumstances, he argues that collectivization is not suggested, even for the usual "market failure" reasons, because competitive sellers of the good will offer their services, unit by unit, to the common demanders and they bid prices down to such an extent that an oversupply rather than an undersupply will be generated. Here collectivization as an alternative institutional form might arise for reasons just opposite to those presumed relevant in the orthodox treatment. This model seems to be of limited relevance in the general case, but it may be applicable to particular kinds of public goods, notably those relating to research and education. This summary is offered as my own interpretation of Earl Thompson's complex analytical model [*The Perfectly Competitive Allocation of Collective Goods,* MR-49, Institute of Government and Public Affairs, University of California, Los Angeles, September 1965].

Neither in this book nor in most of the recent discussion is a distinction made between public goods as consumption goods, and public goods as intermediate goods that enter into the production of final private goods. The theory, in its essentials, is not modified, but this distinction has been precisely formulated by Keimei Kaizuka ["Public Goods and Decentralization of Production," *Review of Economics and Statistics,* XLVII (February 1965), 118–20].

10. Toward a Positive Theory of Public Finance

Introduction

Public finance is now an exciting field of scholarship for a very simple reason. Scholars have only recently begun to look at fiscal phenomena "through a different window." Much remains obscure, but new insights are appearing. New relationships are being derived; old and established institutions and ideas are being subjected to critical analysis. Paradigms have not yet emerged to fix irrevocably the thought patterns of professionals. The theory of public goods remains in a preparadigm stage of development.

Why do we witness the blossoming of this theory only in the mid-twentieth century? In the early and mid-nineteenth century when laissez-faire served as an intellectual model for social order, few intellectual historians should have expected a theory of public goods to parallel the development of the theory of private goods. But why was such a theory absent later from the many and varied proposals for socialist alternatives? Central to socialist reform from the outset and in all its varieties has been the shifting of goods from private or market organization to public or governmental-political organization. Why did the socialist theorists neglect the allocative norms for public provision, and, when these were discussed, why did they limit analysis to private goods, publicly provided? Why do the most sophisticated socialist solutions mirror those of the perfectly working market economy, exclusively characterized by private goods?

These questions, and other similar ones that could be raised, can only be answered in part and guessed at in the large. Socialist and nonsocialist scholars alike tended to accept the dichotomy between the public and the private sectors of the economy. Socialist proposals aimed at shifting the private production of private goods to collective management. Few questions were raised about "public" supply of "public" goods, for the most part, those which had been collectivized from the outset. This sector was not, presumably, subject to economic analysis; it received little attention from socialists or nonsocialists. In this sector, decisions were presumed to be made "politically" and not to be subjected to the analysis applied to decisions on the demand and supply of private goods, whether these should be provided in markets or by governments.

In the political sphere, no attempt was made to relate outcomes to individual values, and policy analysis proceeded on the "as if" assumption of benevolent despotism. This policy presumption was maintained, surprisingly, throughout the very period of history when the extension of suffrage made democratic choice apparent to everyone. From our vantage point, the blindness of the neoclassical English utilitarians to the realities of political democracy must remain largely unexplainable. This was fostered to an extent at least by the accompanying dominance of idealist notions in political theory.

These comments are fully applicable only to the English-American tradition. Continental scholars were more enlightened. Wicksell dominates the scene and he remains the intellectual father of modern public-finance theory. In his perceptive linking of the economics of public finance to the actualities of democratic process, he was at least a half-century in advance of his professional colleagues. The Italians were less sophisticated than Wicksell, but, in Francesco Ferrara, who wrote in the 1850s and 1860s, they take the place of antecedence. Mazzola, Pantaleoni, de Viti de Marco, Einaudi, Barone, Fasiani: these are but a few of the outstanding names in a following Italian tradition that was based on a recognition of the productivity of public services to individuals, on the identity of the producers and consumers of public services in an effectively democratic model, and on the cold realities of exploitation through governmental-fiscal processes. These scholars were almost wholly spared the nonsense of utilitarian pleasure-machines, and they paid little attention to the Edgeworthian vision of measured sacrifice doled out by some omniscient fiscal brain. German-language scholarship should also be mentioned here because of the work of Sax, although his ambiguities concerning collective wants tend to overwhelm the real insights that he possessed. Finally, the Swedes span the era of continental classicism in the work of Erik Lindahl, who, although he was influenced by Wicksell, tended to concentrate attention unduly on the bargained solution to the public-goods problem and to shift attention away from the political-economic relationship properly stressed by Wicksell.

The failures of English-language neoclassical thought in public finance cannot be excused, nor can that of post-Lindahl continental thought. Marshallian economics had its Marshall, who, despite his own reformist urges, was yet able to cut through the normative underbrush and make genuinely scientific progress. Public-finance economists were left to flounder in the muddy mixture of incidence theory and nonsense norms, having no Marshall, and having neither read, nor if read, understood, Wicksell and the Italians. They continued blithely to ignore the whole political process. They remained unconcerned with the way fiscal decisions actually get made, and they were apparently quite willing to define the whole expenditure side of the budget as being outside the pale of their analysis.

It is but small wonder that little progress was made toward either an acceptable normative theory or a positive predictive theory of public finance until near the close of the interwar period. Musgrave's discussion of Lindahl's model, along with Howard Bowen's examination of voting and resource allocation, mark the beginnings of the modern era. These contributions were supplemented and the scope of theory expanded by Paul Samuelson's rigorous formulations of the efficiency conditions in his 1954 and 1955 papers. Wicksell was made available to English-language scholars in translation only in 1958, along with other important continental writers. Only in the decade since have we begun to witness a flowering of interest in public-goods theory, generally, and this interest has not yet reached its zenith.

The Normative Theory of Public Goods

Normative and positive strands are closely intermingled in the modern theory of public goods. As I suggested in Chapter 1, my own interpretation differs from that of other scholars largely in my somewhat greater emphasis on the positive content that can emerge from the analysis; this explains my greater interest in analyzing political choice. In any case, it seems useful to separate the normative and positive elements to the extent that is possible, despite the fact that the analysis is parallel in many of its particulars. The difference arises in the conceptual uses to which the analysis is to be put.

The normative theory of public goods, best represented in the two basic papers by Samuelson, stems directly from theoretical welfare economics. This subdiscipline is widely acknowledged to be normative in that its allocative norms prescribe the ends or "shoulds" of policy, provided that efficiency criteria are accepted. These norms are, of course, much more carefully circumscribed than were those of the old welfare economics. The formal structure of the new version was developed only in the 1930s and 1940s, although the intellectual origins lie in the work of Pareto. After 1934, when Robbins laid bare the weaknesses of the normative presuppositions of the post-Marshallian utilitarians, the search for more rigorous criteria for making policy statements culminated in a rediscovery and elaboration of the Pareto norms for optimality or efficiency. This set of norms allowed economists to classify positions, or proposals for changes in positions, into two separate categories: optimal (efficient) and nonoptimal (inefficient). This classification is accomplished with minimal ethical commitment, and the commitment that is required is such as to command near-universal consent.

In a formal sense, the Pareto constructions were highly useful, and remain so, but economists were not fully satisfied with the formal limits. They sought to find more direct application, and this search produced its own exhausting and long-continuing discussion of compensation. This digression aside, however, the multiplicity of possible outcomes that satisfy Pareto norms in other than the uniquely competitive structures disturbed those who searched for the single best state of the world. This led, in its turn, to the attempts to formulate a "social welfare function," a fictional device that draws attention away from the explicit resort to external and nonindividualistic criteria that is required for any selection from among a set of optimal positions or moves. The basic inconsistency between this and the whole Paretian edifice was either not appreciated or deliberately ignored.

This is an ambiguity that continues to plague modern welfare economics, and with it, the normative theory of public goods. The proper concern of the latter should be limited to laying down the necessary marginal conditions for the allocation of resources to public-goods supply. This task is done when these conditions are formally stated, provided that we disregard the more complex extensions to institutional efficiency discussed in Chapters 8 and 9. It should not be disturbing that distributional questions, described either in terms of some initial imputation of income-wealth or in terms of specific gains-from-trade in public goods, remain unresolved when the allocational norms are stated. Multiple outcomes are possible, each of which will satisfy the conditions for efficiency, but the role of the analysis in this normative version is not that of making a specific selection from among these outcomes. Rather its role is that of providing the formal classification scheme that allows the analyst to place all possible outcomes into one of the two sets.

Both Samuelson and Musgrave fail to sense what to me seems to be the basic contradiction between the social welfare function approach and the use of Pareto criteria. Samuelson defines the necessary conditions for allocative efficiency with respect to public goods, but after having done so, he then resorts to a social welfare function to select the single best state of the world. It is impossible, of course, to isolate the allocative problem from the distributional one, since the sharing of the inframarginal gains-from-trade as well as the initial position will determine allocative outcomes through the operation of income-effect feedbacks. Conceptually, however, this presents no issue since, in my view, the normative theory should end with its formal statement of the necessary conditions that must be met. Musgrave follows a pattern similar to Samuelson's when he conceptually separates the allocation and distribution functions of the budget. It is difficult to understand the logic of this segmentation if a consistent analytical model is desired. If external criteria are introduced to resolve distributional issues, to produce some unique outcome, why should norms based exclusively on individual preference orderings be honored in allocating resources to public-goods production and supply? Since the distribution will, in itself, have feedback effects on allocative outcomes, is not such a separation empty?

My interpretation is that one can present a consistent normative theory of public goods which derives allocative-efficiency conditions from individual preference orderings and which makes no attempt to select from among the set of Pareto-optimal outcomes. The search for a unique solution is misleading since the multiplicity of optima is a characteristic of all interaction processes where gains-from-trade are possible. The apparent uniqueness present under perfectly competitive conditions in the private-goods market should be treated as a bizarre exception, not as a characteristic to be mirrored in other settings.

By classifying this theory as normative, I do not suggest that explicit value judgments are involved or even that the analysis lacks positive content. My usage of the designation "normative" implies that the objective of analysis is to lay down the "should" criteria for resource allocation, given the presumed acceptance of efficiency norms. Much of orthodox economic theory is normative in this sense, oriented to providing "government" with "advice" as to the "shoulds" of economic policy, presuming that efficient resource allocation is desired. In the context of my discussion, the contrast between "normative" and "positive" theory is not one between explicit value espousal and objective or detached analysis. Instead the contrast is one between two sets of objective analysis, the first aimed primarily at specifying precisely the characteristics of results that "should" be aimed for in governmental action on the presumption that efficiency is desired, and the second aimed primarily at *explaining* and *predicting* the outcomes of collective decision processes involving the participation of many persons.

The possibility of separating these two strands of analysis is greater in the theory of public goods than in the theory of private goods, the analysis of markets. In the latter, thorough analysis of the necessary conditions that must be satisfied for overall allocative efficiency carries with it a parallel analysis of the interaction processes through which the voluntary exchange behavior of individuals produces efficient outcomes, given that the familiar set of side conditions is also met. Micro-economic theory becomes at one and the same time a normative theory of public policy to the extent that efficiency objectives are paramount, and a positive theory of market interaction. In the former, the theory conceptually tells the government what conditions should be satisfied; in the latter, the theory predicts the results that will tend to emerge.

In the ordinary normative version of the theory of public goods the positive content is largely contained in its implied prediction concerning what will not happen. The normative theory states the necessary conditions that should be met if the relevant decision makers accept overall efficiency criteria. It does not contain in the process an explanation or prediction about the voluntary interaction of individuals operating to meet these conditions. Quite the opposite; the theory more or less directly implies the positive statement that these voluntary interactions will not meet efficiency requirements, even in some acceptably proximate sense. In other words, the normative theory of public finance contains a positive statement about "market failure" in the presence of public goods. It stops short of analyzing the institutional processes that might be required to generate efficient outcomes.

The Positive Theory of Public-Goods Supply

A positive theory of public finance must begin with the basic efficiency analysis that is contained in the standard normative theory. In addition, it must incorporate the negative result that wholly voluntary behavior of individuals in exchange may not produce outcomes satisfying allocative efficiency requirements. Beyond these essentials, a positive theory must analyze the behavior of persons as they examine organizational alternatives to markets, along with their behavior as they participate in collective decision processes that may be designed to secure mutual gains-from-trade in public goods.

The possible failure of voluntary exchange or market mechanisms to generate efficient outcomes arises because of the large-number setting in which individuals find themselves. The free-rider dilemma expresses this critical feature. Despite the presence of this dilemma, however, there exist mutual gains-from-trade in public goods and services, and these motivate individuals to seek agreements or changes in the rules governing behavior, even if there is no incentive for them to engage in person-to-person bilateral exchanges of the ordinary sort. Before such generalized agreements can be properly analyzed on their own account, small-number models may be introduced *provided* that these are interpreted as useful analogues to large-number models. It is in this context that the small-number models are presented early in this book. These allow us to develop the basic elements of the normative theory in a positive context. The models show that, in the absence of the large-number problem, efficient outcomes will tend to emerge from voluntary-exchange processes. Through these models the theory of public-goods supply is placed in a position roughly comparable to the theory of private goods which, in this respect, remains always in small-number settings.

The models of bilateral (and later of trilateral) trade or agreement on the supply and financing of public goods are not intended to explain real-world fiscal structures. They should be considered as demonstrations of the pressures that mutual gains-from-trade will exert on persons, who will on the basis of their own preferences organize "public-goods trades," save as they are prevented from so doing by the large-number dilemma. In this particular aspect, the bilateral models developed by Lindahl, although they are formally similar to those developed in this book, seem to have been misinterpreted, even by some of their expositors. These models should never have been aimed at explaining how voluntary exchange might lead to efficient outcomes in the presence of public-goods phenomena. Properly interpreted, they show how and why efficient outcomes will emerge, given public-goods phenomena, *in the absence of the large-number dilemma.* In this context, the small-number models represent helpful abstractions in a whole chain of related theoretical reasoning. Much of the criticism of the Lindahl-type models has concentrated on the bargaining or strategic-behavior difficulties encountered in small-number interactions. The attempt of individuals to conceal their own preferences in such situations has been discussed at some length. This line of criticism is, in my opinion, misdirected because it treats the small-number setting as a conceptually real situation, and not as an analytical device that is helpful in extension to large-number situations. If public-goods phenomena should arise only in small groups, and if the analysis of the response of individuals in such groups should be the object of ultimate interest, both the Lindahl-type models and the criticisms of these would serve quite a different function from that under discussion in this book. The primary task of theory is to explain behavior in the presence of public-goods phenomena over large-number groups. Here, the small-number models should, and must, abstract from the specific characteristics of behavior that arise *only* in small-number interactions. If they do not do this, these models can be of no use in explaining the large-number models that must finally be developed.

The simple trading models demonstrate only that efficient outcomes will tend to emerge in the extremely rarefied conditions imposed. If the number of persons is small, and if they behave *vis-à-vis* other persons as if they are in large-number circumstances, ordinary exchange will generate outcomes that may be classified as optimal. The free-rider analysis, following hard on these trading models, demonstrates that the extension of numbers is sufficient to eliminate the optimality properties of predicted trading outcomes. The next stage of a positive theory is apparent. Individuals, recognizing the failure of voluntary-exchange organization, but also continuing to recognize the presence of mutual gains-from-trade in public goods, may propose "rules changes" that will so modify the conditions for individual choice as to secure at least some if not all of the gains-from-trade that are promised. This stage involves the logical derivation of "fiscal systems" as a part of the whole political order from the basic preference orderings of individuals.

The "constitutional rules" that describe the fiscal system must include rules concerning the making of budgetary choices in all aspects. These must include rules for deciding among alternative proposals that might be presented, rules for selecting which goods and services are to be supplied publicly rather than privately, rules for determining the characteristics and the extent of provision for those goods and services that are to be privately supplied, and, finally, rules for allocating the costs of these publicly supplied goods and services among individuals and groups in the whole community.

The mere enumeration of these different sets of rules or institutions suggests the magnitude of the task required before the construction of any complete positive theory. The simple efficiency norms provided by the orthodox Pareto criteria are no longer directly applicable. At another level, efficiency criteria can be evoked, as suggested in some of the earlier discussion, but these are more complex. An extension of Pareto criteria to the predicted operation of rules or institutions becomes possible, and, in one sense, the standard normative theory of public goods can be extended in this manner. This extension goes beyond the problems of determining how much and which public goods should be supplied and moves toward the problems of determining which set of fiscal institutions should be selected. The extended normative theory involves the discussion of the optimal or efficient fiscal constitution.

This extension of theory to the analysis of alternative rules or institutions is more natural in a positive than in a normative approach. In the former, the extension of analysis to the problems of choice among rules becomes an essential follow-on stage. With the normative theorist, having completed his derivation of the required efficiency conditions, there is the underlying presumption that the collectivity, the government, will somehow implement his implied recommendations, or, at the least, will take these into account in the policy mix that it does finally select. With the positive theorist, there is no such underlying presumption since the collectivity simply does not exist apart from the individuals that make up the community. Collective action must be "explained" and "understood" through individual behavior. The questions that must be asked are: How do publicly supplied goods and services get organized in large-number groups? Who decides, and on what basis, which goods and services are to be publicly supplied? Who decides, and on what basis, how much of each good and service to provide? Who decides, and on what basis, how costs are to be shared among members of the community? Who decides, finally, on who is to decide?

There are two separate parts of this institutional stage of a positive theory of public finance. The first consists in the development of a logical theory of individual choice among alternative institutions. This is closely akin to the economist's standard theory of individual choice, and it creates no conceptual difficulties. The procedure here is one of examining the choice among alternative institutional structures in terms of an individual decision calculus. Given a utility function that satisfies the usual conditions, how would an individual order alternative rules and institutions through which certain goods and services will be supplied publicly? To answer this question, even at this logical stage, requires that predicted working properties of alternative institutions be analyzed. The models of Chapters 8 and 9 do little more than to suggest the sort of theorizing that is needed.

The second part of a theory of institutional choice, as an integral part of a positive theory of public finance, is essentially empirical. Perceptive observations of real-world fiscal structures are needed, and the analyst must try to isolate the central elements in such structures that serve best to explain and predict. Conceptually, models of real-world institutions can be tested; hypotheses can be refuted, and, in turn, different hypotheses can be suggested. Painstaking accumulation of the record of historical experience, careful presentation of descriptive detail, and comparative analysis: these are all necessary.

Conclusion

This small book does not contain a complete theory of public finance in the positive sense idealized. This should be emphasized, and no claims in this direction are advanced. Hopefully, I have been able to clarify some of the ambiguities in the elementary stages of analysis. At the same time, I hope that more interesting avenues for further and more complex theory-building have been exposed. If broad agreement among specialized scholars can be attained concerning the theory of public goods in the limited one-good, one-period model, progress will have been considerable. This is true whether these scholars work within either the normative or positive version of analysis. From this limited base, further elaboration and development of the theory of fiscal institutions can take place.

There seems to be no need for a normative-positive clash on methodological principle here. The normatively oriented economist who remains within the Pareto-efficiency framework and who is willing to stretch his constructions beyond their normal limits can be of great assistance to his positivist counterpart who explicitly rejects global efficiency criteria and seeks to predict the results of individual behavior in institutional constraints. The distinction between these two need not lie in the particulars of analysis; the distinction lies instead in the somewhat greater willingness of the normativist to stop short of full explanation, to consider his strict role as "economist" finished once he has completed what, to the positivist "political economist," seems only a part of the job.

In conclusion, I return to the first paragraph of this chapter. The theory of "The Demand and Supply of Public Goods" remains in a preparadigm stage of development. Herein lies its current interest. Also for this reason, no single treatment or presentation is likely to command universal assent among informed scholars nor is it likely to be free of its own ambiguities, confusions and contradictions. This book is surely no exception. It is based on my current (February 1967) interpretation of the central subject matter. On the basis of my own experience in discussing these materials in graduate seminars for more than a decade, I can make only one prediction with certainty. My own views and interpretation in 1977 will not be in full accord with those presented in this book.

Supplementary Reading Materials

In the Preface I noted that this book represents a written version of discussions carried on over a decade in my graduate seminar at the University of Virginia. An appropriate addition to the text may be a listing of reading materials that students in the seminar were assigned as supplementary to the discussion. These are indicated below. Note that some general material is included in this listing that is not contained in the specific references to the literature at the end of the earlier chapters of the book. Similarly, note also that some of the more specific references included in the bibliographical appendices are not included in this general listing.

BOOKS

American Economic Association, *Readings in the Economics of Taxation,* edited by R. A. Musgrave and C. Shoup (Homewood: Richard D. Irwin, 1959).

Kenneth J. Arrow, *Social Choice and Individual Values* (New York: John Wiley and Sons, 1951; Revised edition, 1963).

William J. Baumol, *Welfare Economics and the Theory of the State* (Cambridge: Harvard University Press, 1952; Revised second edition, 1965).

Duncan Black, *The Theory of Committees and Elections* (Cambridge: Cambridge University Press, 1958).

Duncan Black and R. A. Newing, *Committee Decisions with Complementary Valuation* (London: William Hodge, 1951).

Howard Bowen, *Toward Social Economy* (New York: Rinehart, 1948), pt. IV.

James M. Buchanan, *Fiscal Theory and Political Economy* (Chapel Hill: University of North Carolina Press, 1960).

———, *Public Finance in Democratic Process* (Chapel Hill: University of North Carolina Press, 1967).

James M. Buchanan and Gordon Tullock, *The Calculus of Consent* (Ann Arbor: University of Michigan Press, 1962).

Anthony Downs, *An Economic Theory of Democracy* (New York: Harper, 1957).

J. de V. Graaf, *Theoretical Welfare Economics* (Cambridge: Cambridge University Press, 1957).

International Economic Association, *Classics in the Theory of Public Finance*, edited by R. A. Musgrave and A. T. Peacock (London: Macmillan, 1958).

R. A. Musgrave, *The Theory of Public Finance* (New York: McGraw-Hill, 1959).

Mancur Olson, *The Logic of Collective Action* (Cambridge: Harvard University Press, 1965).

MONOGRAPHS

M. Z. Kafoglis, *Welfare Economics and Subsidy Programs*, University of Florida Monographs in Social Science, No. 11, Summer 1961.

Charles Plott, *Generalized Equilibrium Conditions Under Alternative Exchange Institutions*, Research Monograph No. 9, Thomas Jefferson Center for Political Economy, University of Virginia, December 1964.

Earl Thompson, *The Perfectly Competitive Allocation of Collective Goods*, MR-49, Institute of Government and Public Affairs, University of California, Los Angeles, September 1965.

ARTICLES

James M. Buchanan and Milton Z. Kafoglis, "A Note on Public Goods Supply," *American Economic Review*, LIII (June 1963), 403–14.

James M. Buchanan and Gordon Tullock, "Public and Private Action Under Reciprocal Externality," in *The Public Economy of Urban Communities*, edited by J. Margolis (Resources for the Future, 1965).

Otto A. Davis and Andrew Whinston, "Some Foundations of Public Expenditure Theory," Mimeographed. Carnegie Institute of Technology, November 1961.

J. G. Head, "Public Goods and Public Policy," *Public Finance*, XVII (No. 3, 1962), 197–221.

———, "Lindahl's Theory of the Budget," *Finanzarchiv*, XXIII (October 1964), 421–54.

———, "The Welfare Foundations of Public Finance Theory," *Rivista di diritto finanziario e scienza delle finanze* (May 1965), 3–52.

———, "On Merit Goods," *Finanzarchiv*, XXV (March 1966), 1–29.

Leif Johansen, "Some Notes on Lindahl's Theory of Determination of Public Expenditures," *International Economic Review*, IV (September 1963), 346–58.

Paul A. Samuelson, "The Pure Theory of Public Expenditure," *Review of Economics and Statistics,* XXXVI (November 1954), 387–89.

———, "Diagrammatic Exposition of a Theory of Public Expenditure," *Review of Economics and Statistics,* XXXVII (November 1955), 350–56.

———, "Aspects of Public Expenditure Theories," *Review of Economics and Statistics,* XL (November 1958), 332–37.

———, "Pure Theory of Public Expenditure and Taxation," Mimeographed, July 1966.

Robert H. Strotz, "Two Propositions Related to Public Goods," *Review of Economics and Statistics,* XL (November 1958), 329–31.

Author Index

Subject Index

ability-to-pay: theory of taxation, 158
agreement: analysis of, 104, 108, 121, 123, 124, 128, 135–36; collective, cost of, 144–46; collective, process of, 121; collective, theory of, 126; on fiscal rules, 152

bargaining: game, 77, 89; role of, in determining position on contract loans, 102; in determining share in public-goods production, 17
benefit principle of taxation, 157
budget: changes in size of, 36
budgeting: general-fund, 75

club: emergence of, 170; -type goods and services, 170
collective choice: objects of, 121; process of, 130–31, 140; rules for, 174; theory of, 117
collective decision-making, 92, 93; individual participation in, 138–39; in large groups, 109, 185; and market organization, 138–39
comparative advantage: determining efficient trading arrangements, 15–16, 19
competitive economic order: characteristic of, 79; emergence of, in markets, 77
concealing of preferences, 81
consumer's surplus, 24, 39

cooperative group: formation of, 169
cost: of exploiting dissident minorities, 150; of group decision-making, 144–46, 148–52; of multilateral agreements *vis-à-vis* bilateral ones, 9; of negotiating agreements, 22, 169; of *n*-person agreements, 10, 80
cyclical majority problem, 99, 115. *See also* majority

delegation-of-decision rule, 103, 107
divisibility spectrum (scale): arraying of goods along, 163, 168, 178

education: consumption externality in, 64–69, 73; publicly financed, 36
efficiency: conditions for, 45; of final equilibrium, 45; in joint production, 60; least-price-distortion as norm for, 157; normative implications of, 8; orthodox criteria of, 69; pressure toward, 169; in private-goods world, 6, 7; promotion of, by money commodity, 74; in public-goods world, 7, 149, 185; from voluntary exchange process, 7
equilibrium, independent adjustment: attainment of, 16; attainment of under exchange agreement, 15; nonoptimality of, 15; process of establishment of, 16; why and how trade takes place starting from, 25

This book is set in Minion, a typeface designed by Robert Slimbach specifically for digital typesetting. Released by Adobe in 1989, it is a versatile neohumanist face that shows the influence of Slimbach's own calligraphy.

This book is printed on paper that is acid-free and meets the requirements of the American National Standard for Permanence of Paper for Printed Library Materials, z39.48-1992. ∞

Book design by Louise OFarrell, Gainesville, Fla.
Typography by Impressions Book and Journal Services, Inc., Madison, Wisc.
Printed and bound by Edwards Brothers, Inc., Ann Arbor, Mich.